THE
SMALL
BUSINESS
ACTION KIT

THE
SMALL
BUSINESS
ACTION KIT

Third Edition

Written by business counsellors John Rosthorn, Andrew Haldane, Edward Blackwell and John Wholey; edited by Arthur Dicken, Bill Hood, Arthur Mottershead and John Rosthorn, all at Macclesfield Business Ventures.

KOGAN
PAGE

The Small Business Action Kit was written primarily by MBV's business counsellors John Rosthorn, Andrew Haldane, Edward Blackwell and John Wholey. It was edited by MBV's Chairman, Secretary, Treasurer and Director respectively: Arthur Dicken of ICI Pharmaceuticals Division, Bill Hood of William Hood & Co, solicitors, Arthur Mottershead of Josolyne & Co, chartered accountants, and John Rosthorn of ICI Pharmaceuticals Division. The Editorial Committee would like to acknowledge the generous help provided by MBV sponsors and many friends who have contributed material included in the text. The advice and financial help provided by a sister agency – Business Link at Halton – have been much appreciated.

First published in 1986
Second edition 1988, reprinted 1989
Third edition 1991

Kogan Page Limited
120 Pentonville Road
London N1 9JN

British Library Cataloguing in Publication Data

A CIP record for this book is available from the British Library.

ISBN 0-7494-0625-9

Typeset by DP Photosetting, Aylesbury, Bucks.
Printed and bound in Great Britain by Biddles Limited, Guildford.

Contents

Macclesfield Business Ventures (MBV) was set up as a local enterprise agency in 1983. It is sponsored in cash and in kind by the following:

Akusta UK Ltd
Ashton-Vernon Ltd
Barclays Bank plc
British Aerospace plc
British Rail
British Telecom
Cheshire Building Society
Cheshire County Council
Ciba-Geigy plc
Contour Computer Consultants
Cranfield School of Management
R Cressy & Son Ltd
Daniels
Gradus Ltd
Heywood Shepherd
ICI Pharmaceuticals
Josolyne & Co
Lancashire and Cheshire
   County Newspapers

Lightnin' Mixers Ltd
Macclesfield Borough Council
Macclesfield Chamber of Commerce
Macclesfield College of Further
   Education
Macclesfield Community News
Macclesfield Groundwork Trust
Magic Computer Graphics Co
McCann Erickson, Manchester
Midland Bank plc
National Westminster Bank plc
NNC Ltd
Refuge Assurance plc
Robinson Sellars Partners Ltd
Royal Bank of Scotland
Shell UK Ltd
The Boots Company plc
William Hood & Co

MBV exists to help the generation of business growth in small businesses in the Borough of Macclesfield. Its address is Venture House, Cross Street, Macclesfield, Cheshire SK11 7PG.

Introduction

Fifteen hundred business counselling interviews provided the information on which the first edition of this book was based. Following the success of the first edition of *The Small Business Action Kit*, the publication of this second edition, in a revised form, will, it is hoped, enable an even larger readership access to its contents. The essential fabric of the text has been retained in this second edition.

The explanations, summaries and specimen work sheets are designed for use by business counsellors, ranging from those in the professions to those involved in voluntary counselling. The content is arranged to meet the specific needs of business clients labouring under a problem or with an opportunity; it will provide useful leads for counsellors and their clients who will probably need professional assistance in order to reap the greatest benefit from the material. Ideally, each new start-up should have its own copy and use it as a guide, designing its own work sheets from the examples provided.

Every endeavour has been made to ensure accuracy at the time of going to press, including a full review, but readers are reminded that new legislation is passed and regulations changed through the daily activities of Parliament.

John Rosthorn

1

Am I Up to Running My Own Business?

Introduction

For most adults, there are but three options where work is concerned: unemployment, employment and self-employment.

Unemployment	
Advantages	Disadvantages

Employment	
Advantages	Disadvantages

Self-employment	
Advantages	Disadvantages

Using the grids on page 13, rule up a sheet of paper and write down the advantages and disadvantages of each in your own circumstances.

This book is mainly concerned with the successful establishment and expansion of self-employment which will in turn provide employment opportunities for others.

Ideas for business

While there are a few 'ideas' magazines and consultants around, most would-be businessmen have to think up the ideas that would suit them.

Business ideas may be generated through two routes, inspirational and analytical.

1. Inspirational
- A gap in the market-place not satisfied by existing suppliers.
- A new solution to an existing problem; an invention, a process or method.

2. Analytical
Write *your* high interest and high skills factors in the boxes provided.

What businesses match your high scores?

The seven stages of business start-up

These seven points are designed to help you find where you are, and therefore to see what remains to be done.

At which stage are you?
Tick box when stage is completed.

1. *Acquiring motivation.* Finding the urge and energy to pursue the goal of setting up a business. Checking your own personal capability. *Do you have what it takes?* □

2. *Finding an idea* on which it seems reasonable to spend *time* and *money* taking further. □

3. *Proving the idea.* Design and manufacture of samples. Testing the product/service technically and with customers. Testing the market. Understanding the market. Protecting the product/ service by patents and registered design. □

4. *Knowing what is needed.* Developing the framework for getting into business: □

   • Premises, cash, equipment, labour.
   • The time needed to assemble all the resources.
   • Adequate quality control.
   • Professional help in starting a business plan (see page 80).

5. *Under starter's orders.* Applying the business plan. Negotiating for finance, premises, contracts, subcontracts etc. Choosing business name, brand names, the structure (type of company) and registering them. Tax considerations. Use of professional advisers. Getting the right staff. Preparing publicity. □

6. *The 'off'.* First manufacture, first sale. Launch publicity. □

7. *Staying the course.* Keeping track of results. Compare with business plan. Keeping a grip on things. Organising the work. Watching for changes in the market and the law. Keeping the workforce, customers and suppliers happy. Anticipating snags. Improving the product. Looking at competitors. □

Note carefully how much more still remains to be done.

Personal preparation

While this checklist is designed to encourage new business start-ups, it also highlights areas where you are apparently ill equipped. Check your answers with your spouse and your business partner.

Yes or No

1. Are your physical health and age compatible with your proposed project?

2. Can you cope mentally with the new stresses and demands?

3. Do you welcome:
   - calculated risks?
   - and responsibility?

4. Have you demonstrated management ability?

5. Do you have the quality of endurance?

6. Can you work alone for sustained periods?

7. Can you accept a reduced income?

8. Will you work without normal financial security?

9. Are you self-confident in the face of adversity and rebuffs?

10. Do you know how many hours per week you wish to work?

11. Do you know how supportive your wife/husband will be?

12. Have you discussed the project with:
   - her/him?
   - the children?

13. Do you appreciate what effect it could have on:
   - family life?
   - the family home?
   - other assets?

14. Have you listed your personal skills?

15. Do you know well the business you are going into?

Yes or No

16. Can you identify what your business project will need from you?

17. Do you know why you want to start the project?

18. Have you set out truthfully what you want out of the business, and when?

19. Will your project affect your personality?

20. Do you know what your attitude is towards
    - paying taxes?
    - long working hours?
    - selling?
    - asking for money?
    - asking for help?
    - power?
    - success?
    - failure?

21. Are there religious, social, educational, or ethical limitations on your business performance?

22. Can you take decisions?

23. Do you get on with people?

24. Have you realistically listed your personal attributes and shortcomings?

25. Will you discuss this listing with an honest and respected friend?

Press on to the next stage of the project if you have truthfully answered 'Yes' to almost every question.

If most of your answers are 'No', perhaps you should think again about trying to start your own business.

Initial preparation for the business

Now to the business itself. How much do you know about your business area? Use this checklist:

Yes or No

1. Do you have a clear idea of the business opportunity now facing you?

2. Will your product sell?

3. Do you accurately understand your intended product/service?

4. Have you looked at the market for it?
   - What people buy
   - When they buy it
   - Where they buy it
   - Who does the buying
   - Why they should choose your product/service
   - How you will set about selling yours
   - How big the market is for your product
   - Whether it will grow or contract
   - What your share of the market will be

5. Have you checked the moral, legal and environmental objections to your product?

6. Do you know why your product is best?

7. Can you explain this clearly to customers?

8. Will it remain the best?

9. Does it do what you say it does; has it been tested?

10. Will you continue to improve your product?

11. Do you know where new products will come from?

12. Have you sold your product yet?

13. Are you familiar with what customers want?
    - Delivery and after-sales service requirements
    - Quality levels
    - Discount levels

14. Do you know who your competitors are?

Yes or No

15. Do you know what they will do if you enjoy some success?

16. Can you keep up to date with changing techniques and technology?

17. Have you spoken to any potential customers about the market?

18. Do you know what your product will cost to make?

19. Have you calculated your overheads, including selling and distribution?

20. Have you attempted a simple cash flow projection?

21. At this stage do you have an idea of:
    - How much cash you will need in the next 12 months?
    - How much cash you can personally raise?
    - How much external cash you need?
    - When you can repay it?

22. Have you agreed within the family what security you can offer your financiers?

23. Do your partners/shareholders understand your project?

24. Do you know how much it will cost to publicise your product?

25. Do you have:
    - A solicitor?
    - An accountant?
    - A bank manager?
    - Other essential specialists?

26. Have these specialists been properly briefed about the services you require and replied formally about the cost of the service?

27. Have you identified the problems you have never faced before?

The first phase of setting up in business is only completed when you have truthfully **answered 'Yes' to virtually all these questions.**

19

Cost of living

	Current annual expenses	Economies which can be sustained for a time	Economies which can be made for a lengthy period
Rent or mortgage payments			
Rates			
Food			
Heating, lighting			
House repairs/maintenance			
Personal travel			
Vehicle repairs/maintenance			
Insurances			
Holidays and entertainment			
Clothing			
Subscriptions			
Gifts			
Others —			
—			
—			
TOTAL	£	£	£

Now, how much do you need to earn from your business gross, before income tax and National Insurance?

- Per month £
- Per annum £

Personal and domestic costs have a real bearing on the required financial return from a business venture. Fill in the table and work out how much you will need to earn to pay your way.

The final test

In 1984, a second report on business failure under the Loan Guarantee Scheme was prepared by chartered accountants, Robson Rhodes, 'A Study of Business Finance Under the Small Business Loan Guarantee Scheme', published by the Department of Trade and Industry. The authors highlighted shortcomings in the capabilities of proprietors/managers in small business.

Do you avoid these shortcomings? How well do you understand the following and does your business plan cover them adequately?

- Business finance
- Principal risks to your business
- The competition you will face
- General management of a business
- Marketing
- Production (if applicable)

How strong is your own record of achievement in industry or commerce?

Unless a realistic assessment of your capabilities gives satisfactory answers to these questions, there are two possible courses of action:

1. Abandon the idea.
2. Take steps to correct weak areas *before* starting the business. For example:
   - Enrol on a relevant 'Start a Business' course
   - Engage qualified professional advisers
   - Visit your Local Enterprise Agency or Training and Enterprise Council
   - Find partners/shareholders/employees with the required experience.

2
What Are the Options?

Business start-ups

There is a very limited number of ways of getting into business.

Which best meets the constraints you have in terms of skills, experience, money, property? Has your preferred choice really got a future for you? What about the others?

1. Buy an existing business
2. Buy the assets of a failed business
3. Put together a new business

   (a) Very similar to what is already being done
   (b) Novel or unique product/service

4. Take up a franchise (see page 26)
5. Start a co-operative (see page 28).

In your situation	
Advantages	*Disadvantages*

Buying a business

The ways in which businesses may be acquired are few in number. This chart sets out the major issues upon which professional advice should be taken to minimise the risk of loss or unnecessary expense.

Purchaser	Vendor	Method
Individual, partnership or company	Sole trader, partnership or company	Acquire assets

Watch out for these points
Valuation of fixed assets and stock
Valuation of goodwill
Some assets may not be legally transferable
Transfer of patents, trade marks, licences, copyright and other assets
Service contracts
Vendor responsible for redundancies
Freedom of 'old' management to set up in competition

Purchaser	Vendor	Method
Individual or partnership	Shareholders	Acquire shares

Watch out for these points
Acquired as a going concern, hence:

- Product liability for old defaults
- Existing contracts maintained including employment
- Pension liabilities taken over
- Obtain warranties and indemnities from vendor
- Liability for debts if trading when insolvent
- Control exercised through shareholders*

* A majority shareholding exceeding 50 per cent gives day-to-day control of a company subject to the law of the land and contractual obligations entered into. But some important purposes – notably winding up of the company – require a 75 per cent interest.

Purchaser	Vendor	Method
Company	Shareholders	Acquire shares – for cash – by issue of shares

Watch out for these points
As above for individual or partnership, *plus*
Consolidation of Group Accounts

In an open market, a business is worth what the highest bidder will pay for it. It does not follow that this price is fair, right or moral. LOOK OUT!

Buying a shop

Because Britain is alleged to be a 'nation of shopkeepers', and because most shops fail, it is particularly necessary to question your plans.

1. Why do you want to buy a shop? Name your reasons.
2. What direct competition exists in the area?
3. What indirect competition is there?
   - Mail order
   - Party plan
   - Fairs
   - Markets
4. In the catchment area, what is the:
   - Population
   - Unemployment level
   - Purchasing power

   And their trends?

   What effect might recent or likely changes in these trends have on the business?
5. Is the area to be re-developed?
   (a) Any supermarkets proposed? Will these compete?
   (b) Any road widening or change of traffic flows proposed? Will these affect the business?
   (c) Will the proximity of suppliers change? With what effect?
6. What are, or will be, the main customer types, eg school children for shops near to schools? Any changes likely?
7. How many people pass the shop each day?

   What proportion of them want your intended product range?

   What will be the size of the average purchase?
8. Walk the streets. Talk to neighbouring shopkeepers, customers and your bank's local manager. Read the local newspapers. Find out all you can about trade in the street and the locality.
9. Note dates of ownership of:

current owner	19XX – 19XX	Why is he selling?
prior owner	19XX – 19XX	

   What does this information indicate?

10. What are current:

Sales	£	/week
Purchases	£	/week
Gross margins by product		per cent

Check till rolls.

Check paying-in books, purchase invoices and delivery notes.

Ignore stories of 'cash into the back pocket'.

11. What do the professionally prepared accounts indicate about:

		This year	Last year	Prior year
Sales	£			
Expenses	£			
Profits	£			

Now do your own forecasts.

12. Check rate of staff turnover. How many will stay on with new owner? Can you recruit new staff successfully?

13. Have comparisons with other shops and businesses been made?

14. What would be the value of the freehold or the lease if property were empty?

15. How much will you need to borrow?   £
Will the business support this borrowing?

16. Have you organised advice from accountants, valuers, solicitors?

17. What hours will you have to work?

Calculate $\dfrac{\text{Profit}}{\text{Your annual working hours}} = £$ /hour.

18. Note living accommodation, proximity of schools and churches, recreation facilities, car parks, transport and other social factors.

19. See question 1. Do you still want to buy this shop? If so, write down why.

Also do the calculations on page 28.

Current income versus self-employment

It is easy to suppose that self-employment will bring greater income – it rarely does! Try this exercise to see how your project looks.

A	Enter purchase price of business (excluding stock).	£
B	Enter stock as valued.	£
C	Enter cost of improvements needed, if any.	£
D	Enter any other costs, eg legal fees etc.	£
E	Add A, B, C and D together = Total cost of business.	£
F	Enter *net* profit (pre-tax) including any proprietor's salary in last year of business, but be sure you have deducted the bank or loan interest *you* will have to pay.	£
G	Enter *net* profit (pre-tax) estimated for *next* year including proprietor's salary, but be sure you have deducted the bank or loan interest *you* will have to pay.	£
H	Enter current interest paid on present cash on deposit or other investments to be sold.	£ £
I	Enter your present annual earnings or social security payments.	£
J	Add H and I together.	£
K	Deduct J from F = Benefit from running business (calculated on current earnings).	£
L	K ÷ E × 100 = Return on investment (calculated on current earnings).	%
M	Deduct J from G = Benefit from running business (calculated on estimated earnings).	£
N	M ÷ E × 100 = Return on investment (calculated on estimated future earnings).	%

There are other valid reasons for starting a business. What are yours?

But don't forget these figures.

One option: taking up a franchise

Franchises are growing rapidly. In the UK, the number increased from 2000 to 16,000 between 1978 and 1986, with successful franchises like Body Shop and Dyno-Rod as examples. Franchises have continued to increase in importance as opportunities for new business start-ups. Because they have a much higher survival rate, they are viewed favourably by outside investors, notably the banks.

Setting up a franchise

The franchisor will eventually sell a package of *proven* know-how relating to a specific type of business activity. With the package the franchisor is likely to attract sound franchisees and the necessary finance: 12 months may well be necessary to complete this development programme.

1 .Eliminate as soon as possible the risks inherent in any business start-up by thoroughly market testing a small number of pilot operations.

2. Provide the means by which the franchisee can be his own boss.

3. Develop a detailed operational manual setting out how the business should be run.

4. Develop strong branding of the franchise through media appropriate to the franchise's target market.

5. Prepare the franchise prospectus to show anticipated returns on investment.

6. Obtain Newspaper Publishers Association approval prior to advertising for franchisees (Newspaper Publishers Association Ltd, 16 Took's Court, London EC4A 1LB; telephone 071-405 6806), but this is probably dealt with through the publication you choose.

7. Protect intellectual property: patents, trade marks, copyrights.

8. Prepare the franchise agreement with a solicitor experienced in this field.

9. Obtain in-principle support from the franchise specialist units in the major banks.

10. Consider joining the British Franchise Association: Franchise Chambers, 75a Bell Street, Henley-on-Thames, Oxon RG9 2BD; telephone 0491 578049.

Franchise checklist

1. *Business environment*   *Tick when checked*

(a) Analyse own motivation and capabilities.   ☐

(b) Review commitment of the immediate family to the idea.   ☐

(c) Assess public awareness and acceptability of franchised
    product.   ☐

(d) Check protection of product by patents, trade marks,
    copyrights.   ☐

(e) Look for strong possibility of expanded use of product. ☐

(f) Review strength of competition, franchised or otherwise. ☐

(g) Examine pricing. ☐

2. *Franchisor* *Tick when checked*

(a) Find out length of time and experience in franchising in the UK. ☐

(b) Obtain the bank status report and latest audited accounts. ☐

(c) Look at the management structure. ☐

(d) Review communication systems and effectiveness. ☐

(e) Contact other existing franchisees. ☐

(f) Get comments on operations manual. ☐

(g) Note payments to franchisor: fee, royalty, levy. ☐

3. *Franchise agreement*

(a) Note terms and conditions of renewal. ☐

(b) Look at franchisor's and franchisee's obligations. ☐

(c) Check out franchisor's accountability regarding advertising and other levies. ☐

(d) Examine franchise sale options. ☐

(e) Note minimum sales quantity requirement and other termination clauses. ☐

(f) Understand exclusivity of territories. ☐

(g) Note compulsory death and incapacity covers. ☐

(h) VAT liabilities on fees, royalties etc. ☐

Another option: worker co-operatives

What is a worker co-operative?
A worker co-operative is basically a business owned and controlled by those who work in it.

Each member has an equal say, either in the running of the co-operative, or in the election of a management committee.

Profits are shared by the members in proportion to the work put in by each.

Who starts a worker co-operative?
People with an idea for a marketable product or service, and the skills, experience and enthusiasm needed to work together.

People who want to work for themselves as equals and share the rewards in an equitable way and at the same time create useful employment.

People who want to work locally and keep profits in the community.

People who are unemployed, in danger of becoming so, or in need of part-time work.

Companies that see their employees as partners and wish to improve motivation and job satisfaction can convert to worker co-operatives.

How do you go about it?
The Co-operative Development Agency (CDA) can extend its help to those wanting to set up a worker co-operative. Contact the CDA direct at Broadmead House, 21 Panton Street, London SW1Y 4DR; telephone 071-839 2988, or through the local enterprise agency.

CDA will advise you on what is necessary to get going, discuss the demand for your product or service, help you to draw up a business plan and prepare loan applications, help find suitable premises and guide you through legal and tax matters.

CDA also have available ready-made rules for co-operatives, which have been tried and tested throughout the UK to ease the process of registration.

3

What Has to be Done? Who Will Help?

Countdown to start-up

This list outlines matters to be resolved before a business can start trading. Use the boxes to indicate what you have completed.

Date done See also page

1. Note the addresses and phone numbers of local business advisers such as:

   - Small Firms Service

   - Rural Development Commission

   - Local Enterprise Agency

   - Small Business Club

   Check availability of local courses on starting a business. 42–4

2. Research and understand the market for your product.

3. Establish preliminary product costings. 121–3

4. Review the seven qualifications for the Enterprise Allowance (Jobcentre leaflet). If appropriate, book in for an 'information session' through the Jobcentre. *Don't* start trading until accepted on to the scheme, if you are eligible.

5. Appoint your accountant; agree service and fee. Establish business records systems. 33

6. Appoint your solicitor; agree service and fee. Review the form of your business. 34–5

7. Select business name. 105

Date done See also page

8. Find and cost premises. Consult Fire Brigade about expenses associated with obtaining a Fire Certificate. — 92–3, 97

9. Check with Planning Office, District or Borough Council, about planning and building regulations constraints on the property/home. Note restrictions on the use of advertising signs. — 92, 99–100

10. Advise your bank manager of your plans. — 35

11. Determine what licences, certificates and the like will be necessary to permit you to trade. — 109

12. Investigate patent, registered design, trade mark and copyright protection. Apply for protection if justifiable. — 112–14

13. Check the availability of grant aid for your business. — 88–90

14. Locate key suppliers, confirm their prices and deliveries. — 118

15. Establish your prices and discounts. — 46–9

16. Complete the business plan, including 12-month financial plan. N.B. Ensure business plan includes sufficient cash being available to cover the requirement of the first 12 months. — 80–81

17. Obtain from bank written confirmation of loan/overdraft facilities. Seek to understand how arrangement fees, bank charges and interest will be charged. Open the bank account. — 76, 85–7

18. If applicable, form a company or draw up a partnership agreement. — 102–4

19. For business premises, take professional advice on leases, purchase and licences. — 35–6, 94

20. Apply for and obtain permission to trade where necessary (see also 11 above). — 98, 100

21. Inform Inspector of Taxes that you are starting in business, preferably through your accountant, using Form 41G. Provide him with your P45. Read booklet IR28 'Setting up in Business'. — 108

Date done See also page

22. Inform Department of Social Security (DSS)
for National Insurance purposes. Check
availability of Income Support. [ ] 108, 134–9,
142

23. Establish income tax and National Insurance
contribution deductions using appropriate
forms. Be familiar with Statutory Sick Pay
(SSP) Scheme and Statutory Maternity Pay
(SMP). [ ] 132–9, 143–4

24. Contact VAT Office and, if necessary,
establish records and registration (in
telephone directory under Customs and
Excise). [ ] 107–8, 116

25. Confirm mail and telephone links with Post
Office and British Telecom. [ ] 128–9

26. Plan communications of product/service to
your target market. [ ] 50–59

27. Make sure appropriate insurance covers are
taken out. [ ] 110

28. Establish terms and conditions of
employment. Note the requirement to
maintain existing terms and conditions
where an existing business is being taken
over. [ ] 132–9

29. Contact Jobcentre regarding future
employees. Consider Youth Training
Scheme. [ ] 131

30. Take delivery of all business stationery and
promotional materials. [ ] 50, 115

31. Advise the Rating Department of your
District or Borough Council. Check options
to pay monthly and half yearly. Avoid
paying rates on empty premises and if you
live on your business premises there may be
liability for both council (community) charge
and business rates. Details of the business
rate legislation is available from the
Department of the Environment, FLT
Division, Room N6/20, 2 Marsham Street,
London SW1P 3EB. [ ]

Date done See also page

32. Factories: advise Health and Safety Executive. ☐

33. Shops and offices: complete and return Form OSR 1 to Environmental Health and Housing Department, District or Borough Council. ☐

34. Ensure mains services are connected to your premises:

    ● Gas ☐

    ● Electricity (single/three phase) ☐

    ● Water ☐

    ● Drainage ☐

35. For credit or hire sales, apply to Trading Standards Office. ☐

36. Prepare launch of the business with press/media support. ☐ 50–60

37. Take out bank and credit references for major new, unknown credit customers. Think twice about some known credit customers. ☐ 124

38. Consider joining the:

    ● Small Business Club ☐

    ● Chamber of Commerce, or equivalent ☐

    ● Chamber of Trade ☐

    ● Trade Association, eg Master Builders, Licensed Victuallers ☐

Selection of professional advisers

All small businesses should seek cost-effective contributions to the management of their business from appropriate professional advisers. Key professions include accountants, solicitors, estate agents and bank managers.

The best times to make the choice are:

● before the business begins operations
● before a new phase in the development of the business.

The steps in the selection process are:

1. Make appointments and visit at least two, preferably three, of each class of adviser.

33

2. Discuss your business opportunity. Agree with the adviser the list of services he can provide to meet business needs.

3. Agree the dates by which the services will be provided.

4. Discuss the cost of the service and the terms of payment for it.

5. Obtain confirmation in writing of points 2, 3 and 4.

6. Make your selection on the basis of the written confirmation and the personal interview.

7. Courteously advise the prospective advisers of your choice.

Services available from your advisers

The checklists will help you to see what your advisers can do for you. It is your job to ensure that you get value for money spent on buying their services.

Accountant

Your account should be a vital member of your small management team.

- Company formation
- Partnership agreements
- Accounting/Bookkeeping systems
- Value Added Tax (VAT)
- Pay as you Earn (PAYE)/National Insurance administration
- Government grants
- Business planning including budgets and forecasts
- Cash raising
- Management information
- Interim accounts preparation
- Year-end accounts preparation
- Annual audit
- Capital restructuring
- Business tax
- Business tax planning
- Company secretarial services
- Personal tax
- Personal tax planning
- Pension arrangements/schemes
- Disability arrangements
- Death cover
- Retirement planning
- Investment planning
- Inheritance Tax planning
- Wills
- Receiverships and liquidations

Solicitor

Your solicitor will prove to be of vital importance on occasions during the formation, growth and, perhaps, the winding up of your business. Agree the service(s) to be provided.

- Tailormade company formation and registration
- Partnership agreements. A written agreement covering basic terms is advisable.
- Property – freehold and lease negotiations and conveyancing
- Employment law, eg contracts of employment
- Commercial law, eg agency appointments
- Debt collection
- Inter-company disputes
- Distribution, licensing, secrecy, manufacturing agreements
- Patents and copyright
- Terms of trade
- Personal guarantees.

Bank

Your bank is a very necessary part of your business from the start. A vast organisation of specialists is available to guide you in the financial planning of your business, and on the best use of funds.

A short guide to possible facilities available:

- *Current account.* For day-to-day trading.
- *Deposit account.* For investment of surplus funds – special rates for larger deposits.
- *Loan account* (long term). Capital borrowings repaid over period of years.
- *Assistance in importing and exporting.* Advice on methods, finance; economic intelligence reports on countries worldwide.
- *Provision of finance.* Overdraft, loans, discounting, bills of exchange, medium-term loans, business start-up loans, business expansion loans, government Loan Guarantee Scheme.
- *Leasing/factoring services.* Through specialist bank subsidiaries.
- *Transmission of funds.* Credit transfers, overseas payments, direct debit system etc.

Your local manager is available to give on-the-spot advice in all matters relating to the financial aspect of your business.

Architect

Your architect is a valuable member of the building team in the construction of new premises and the alteration of existing buildings.

His work includes site investigation, feasibility studies, obtaining planning consents, investigation into problems of strength, construction, weather proofing, energy conservation etc.

An architect knows the best way through all the problems and regulations associated with building, and will look after your interests through all or any stages of a building project.

Services supplied by your architect may include:

- *New buildings.* Investigation of site, town planning problems, feasibility studies including estimates of the cost of the project, sketch plans, working drawings, obtaining competitive quotations, preparing contracts, supervising the work to completion.
- *Old buildings.* In addition to the services listed above for new buildings, your architect may be able to complete feasibility studies regarding alterations and improvements.
- *Grant work.* Advising on any grants available.
- *Litigation.* Providing technical expertise in building dispute cases.
- *Energy saving.* Advising on economies in heating of properties and on any grants and other such help available to meet the costs of new installations to achieve energy saving.
- *Advice on leases on purchase of property.* Advice can be given on the conditions attached to purchases on leases, including the preparation of schedules of conditions to be incorporated in any lease.

Services available from a surveyor and most estate agents

Where bank lending is to finance the purchase of a property, the bank will require a valuation of that property by a reputable valuation surveyor. Sometimes banks recommend a valuer; others let you choose your own. If you choose your own, advise the bank of your choice at an early stage. Always choose a member of the Royal Institution of Chartered Surveyors (RICS) or the Incorporated Society of Valuers and Auctioneers (ISVA).

The surveyor will also be able to advise on the following:

If you are buying:

- Structural condition of the property
- Whether or not the rating assessment is too high
- Defective workmanship
- Whether or not planning permission is required and making the application.

If you are leasing:

- The condition of the property and make recommendations. Modern leases usually make the tenant responsible for all repairs; with older buildings the implications can be immense. A surveyor will advise on schedules of condition and negotiate your lease terms.
- Rating
- Planning permission
- Negotiating the rent at the commencement of the lease or upon rent review.

The surveyor will also be able to recommend other associated professions who can give more detailed advice on heating, electrical installations, and building design.

Insurance adviser

Your insurance adviser is important at all stages of your business career, from initial planning onwards. He will help you to ensure the continuation of your business and your income should accidents occurr, and also ensure that you meet any legal requirements, eg public liability insurance.

Certain areas of insurance such as life and pensions require a specialist adviser.

When you seek his advice you should cover the areas listed below. Choose an adviser who is helpful, efficient, and in whom you can trust.

- *General*
  Accident, fire, theft, vehicles, stock, equipment etc

- *Business*
  Liability and consequential loss

- *Sickness*
  Personal accident, temporary/permanent disability, private medical care

- *Death*
  Of key personnel, shareholder, owner or partner

- *Pension*
  Directors, employers, employees
  State, insured and self-administered schemes

- *Loans*
  Alongside pension or pension loanback

- *Personal investment planning*
  Your capital and/or income requirements or
  aims outside direct business growth.

If the insurance covers are to be arranged through a broker, be sure to enquire about the insurance company with which the business is placed. The most reliable service may be provided by members of the British Insurance Association, Aldermary House, Queen Street, London EC4N 1TT; telephone 071-248 4477.

Design consultant

Design has a vital, often misunderstood, role in improving profitability.

1. Will improved design increase my share of the intended, or existing market?

2. Will it reduce manufacturing costs?

3. Will it improve the product?

4. Will it improve cash flow, net of costs?

Where the answer is 'Yes' to these questions, contact a designer, looking for these particular points:

(a) Designer should spend enough time learning about you and your business.

(b) Obtain a 'no obligation' proposal of design work founded on the areas already agreed in discussions.

(c) Ensure your designer submits the proposal accurately describing work to be undertaken, in stages, with time and costs clearly shown.

(d) Brilliance is no substitute for experience, so choose a designer with a track record. Ask for references; discover whether the design experience is suitable to your need.

Then:

(e) Payment should be made only after a satisfactory completion of each stage.

In some cases, design assistance may be available under the Design Council's Design Advisory Service Funded Consultancy Scheme. Details are available from the Design Council, 28 Haymarket, London SW1Y 4SU; telephone 071-839 8000. Otherwise, there is the Design Initiative of the Department of Trade and Industry, information about which is given in a booklet, available by telephoning 0800 500 200, and entitled 'The Enterprise Initiative'.

Public relations consultant

The PR task is to help you devise your company message, to select who receives it, and to make sure that you communicate that company message to the target group in the outside world.

- *Press relations*
  The most common form of PR. Prepare your message, usually in the form of a press release about your product, despatch to the relevant media (newspapers, magazines, trade journals, radio or TV); could involve a press reception or arrange special events to attract media attention.

- *Corporate PR*
  Will help you describe your company to the outside world: could take the form of a company brochure, film or video; may involve research into how other people (eg your suppliers or customers) see you and how to change their views (or yours) for the better.

- *Lobbying*
  Is intended to change the view of a legislative body, eg Parliament, EEC committees, the Town Hall, your union executive, by preparing a case for their consideration. Methods include: arranging special meetings, personal contact, public exposure.

- *Financial PR*
  Is intended to attract investors to your company. Work with brokers and merchant banks to ensure the correct company profile or to attract attention in the specialist financial media.

- *Industrial PR*
  Helps you explain company activities to your employees. It can take the form of a company newsletter, open days, sponsorship of sports teams or local events.

PR for new companies
A new company needs to identify its 'publics'. Who would influence the success of your business? Is it the Town Hall, the local residents, employees, an untapped market, a trade union or a government department?

PR consultancies can help you with a wide variety of marketing and management tasks. Larger companies employ specialists in market research, audio-visual production, management consultancy, promotions and advertising, but a smaller company can get this advice from their PR consultancy. Writing customer letters, sales leaflets or video scripts, for example, is often the area when a PR consultancy is particularly helpful.

Advertising agent
It is probably *more important for a small firm to make effective use of its promotional funds than it is for a large company.* A well chosen and well briefed advertising agency can make a big contribution to this work.

A 'full service' advertising agency will handle:

- *Research.* Market, advertising, pricing, pack
- *Campaign presentation.* Artwork, layout, copy, media, design
- *Implementation.* Production, media buying, delivery, insertions, monitoring of costs and effectiveness
- *Sales promotion.* Pack, deals
- *Merchandising/Display.* Point of sale work
- *Development.* Product, market
- *Forecasting.* Sales, mathematical modelling
- *Exhibitions.* Stand design and management
- *Public relations.* Media, lobbying.

Smaller agencies may handle just one or two of the functions listed.

The small business client should approach his briefing of the advertising on the basis of:

- Knowing the *product benefits*
- Knowing the *target market* – the customer
- Knowing what the advertising must do.

Dealing with your local council

Executives or officials employed by the council have delegated powers enabling them to take decisions which may affect your business. In other cases the powers are retained by sub-committees or the council itself, which may accept or reject advice provided by the officers. To benefit your business you should know who takes the decision and how.

The charts overleaf show typical executive and committee structures in a local council.

Committee structure of a typical District or Borough Council

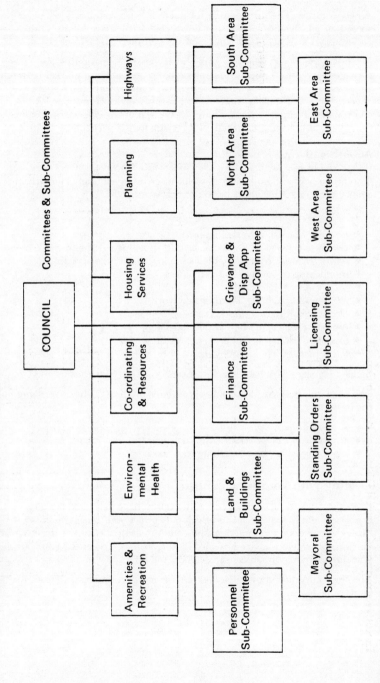

Executive structure of a typical District or Borough Council

4

No Customers – No Business

Market research for the small business

Whatever your talents are, skilled craftsman, top executive, butcher, baker or candlestick maker, all have one thing in common – *no customers, no business.* A vague idea that there are lots of people out there who need me is a pleasant thought and good for the ego – but it won't pay the rent, and it won't convince your bank manager to lend you money.

The way to understand better whether customers truly exist is to ask the right questions:

1. How many *potential customers are there?*
2. *How many real* customers are there?
3. Who are they?
4. Who does the buying?
5. Where is the buying done?
6. Where are the customers?
7. What kind of product or service do they want to buy?
8. Why do they want the product or service?
9. Where do they get it at present?
10. How much will they want to pay?
11. What deficiencies do the current products or services have?
12. When do customers buy, how much and how frequently?
13. Can you deliver what they want when they want it?
14. Who else can supply this product/service?
15. How strong is this competition?
16. Will the market grow or contract?

The answers to questions may be found by:

  (a) *'Desk' research.* Newspapers, advertisements, libraries, reference works, textbooks, market surveys.

(b) *Visiting potential retailers/distributors*. Talking to them in a pre-planned way, finding out prices and discounts.
(c) *Visiting competitors*. Talking to them, obtaining literature, price-lists and samples.
(d) *Observing similar establishments*. Customer flow.
(e) *Visiting users*. Discussing what benefits they associate with your product or product type.

Such contacts may be made by:

- Personal visit – the best.
- Telephone – but only by a skilled person aided by a written guideline.
- Mail questionnaire – but expect a low response.

Part of the market research is quite properly descriptive – 'feel' and is described as *qualitative* research. For analysts such as bank managers and business advisers, there is also a vital requirement for numbers: *quantitative* research.

For would-be retailers, traffic flow into the shop is vital. Research location!

Sources of market information

In the preparation for the business start-up, it can be easy to neglect the opportunity to check published information – often available free of charge – which may allow the market size, trends, prices and customers to be identified.

Agricultural Statistics, HMSO

Annual Abstract of Statistics, HMSO

British Monitors, HMSO

Census of Population, HMSO

County, Borough and Town Profiles, County and District Councils (various)

County Council Industrial Registers, County Councils (various)

Digest of UK Energy Statistics, HMSO

Dun & Bradstreet Directories

Employment Gazette, HMSO

European Marketing Data and Statistics, Euromonitor

Family Expenditure Survey, HMSO

Financial Statistics, HMSO

General Household Survey, HMSO

Inland Revenue Statistics, HMSO

Kelly's Business Directory, Kelly's Directories

Kompass Register, Kompass Publishers

Main Economic Indicators, HMSO

Market Research Great Britain, Euromonitor

Mintel Market Intelligence, Mintel

National Income and Expenditure, HMSO

Regional Trends, HMSO

Social Trends, HMSO

Yellow Pages, British Telecom

Have you visited your local library? Much of this information and more is waiting for you there.

Product pricing

Avoiding the temptation to establish prices on the basis of internal costs, the successful business:

1. Researches prices and discounts in the market

2. Remembers that price is an attribute of the market *and* product or service

3. Assesses other elements in the competition – notably quality and delivery

4. Knows that it is easier to reduce a price than to put it up.

For a conventional manufactured product sold by wholesale and retail distribution, this price schedule may help you to price your product in the market-place.

	Main competitors									Your product	
	1			2			3			Initial price	Adjusted price
	Pack size			Pack size			Pack size				
	A	B	C	A	B	C	A	B	C		
Name of product											
Main retailer											
Recommended retail price											
Marketed price											
Actual selling price											
Trade price* Volume discounts											
Net trade price*											
Wholesale price* Volume discounts											
Net wholesale price*											
Quality rating											
Delivery rating											
Other ratings											

* It may be difficult to get all this information.

Price as an attribute of the product or service

It is too easy, and bad business, to think that the new product or service has to be the cheapest.

This table encourages you to compare your products with your competitors. Tick as appropriate.

Comparison with competitors

Product attributes	Worse			Same	Better			Tick which product attributes are most important to the customer
	-3	-2	-1	0	+1	+2	+3	
Design								
Performance								
Packaging								
Presentation/appearance								
After-sales service								
Availability								
Delivery								
Colour/flavour/ odour/touch								
Image								
Specification								
Payment terms								
Others:								

Now look again at:

Discounts

Price

And now, at your costs

Discounts and price changes

Discounts

Suppliers may offer cash discounts for prompt payment of outstanding bills. Use this table to see how the cost of the deal compares with overdraft or loan interest rates.

	Annual interest rate % to break even (pre-tax) (Cost in %)							
	Extra credit taken – in weeks							
Discount forgone: %	5	6	7	8	9	10	11	12
1	10.5	8.7	7.5	6.6	5.8	5.2	4.8	4.4
1½	15.8	13.1	11.3	9.9	8.8	7.9	7.2	6.6
2	21.1	17.6	15.1	13.2	11.7	10.5	9.6	8.8
2½	26.4	22.0	18.9	16.5	14.7	13.2	12.0	11.0
3	31.8	26.5	22.7	19.9	17.7	15.9	14.4	13.2
5	53.5	44.6	38.2	33.5	29.7	26.8	24.3	22.3

Price reductions

Cut the price to increase sales volume. Before you do, check that sales volume increase needed to break even (ignoring the costs of handling increased sales volumes) really will happen. Beware of setting off a price war with your competitors; it is the route to ruin for you all.

Percentage sales volume increase needed to break even on a price reduction						
	Gross margins (%)					
Price reduction	15	20	25	30	35	40
1%	7.1	5.3	4.2	3.5	2.9	2.6
5%	50.0	33.3	25.0	20.0	16.7	14.3
10%	200.0	100.0	67.7	50.0	40.0	33.3
15%	—	300.0	150.0	100.0	75.0	60.0

Price increases

As a corollary, look at the sales volume reductions which a price increase will support. It is more profitable to sell fewer items at a higher price.

Price increase	Percentage sales volume decrease supported by a price increase					
	Gross margins (%)					
	15	20	25	30	35	40
1%	6.3	4.8	3.9	3.2	2.8	2.4
5%	25.0	20.0	16.7	14.3	12.5	11.1
10%	40.0	33.3	28.6	25.0	22.2	20.0
15%	50.0	42.9	37.5	33.3	30.0	27.3

Marketing

Marketing of products or services is just as important for small businesses as it is for the giant fast-moving consumer goods companies like Procter & Gamble.

Marketing means the consistent, coherent communication of benefits derived from the product or service to the consumer.

	Channels of communication	Customers
	Business name	
	Letterhead	
	Business card	
	Business stationery	DISTRIBUTORS
	Logo	
	Product names	
	Packaging	
	Delivery service	
	Vans	
	Overalls/tunics	
	Price-lists	
	Pricing	
	Discounts	RETAILERS
	Samples/prototypes	
	Editorial coverage	
	Personal selling, sales presentation, folders	
Benefits from the PRODUCT OR SERVICE	Telephone selling	
	Direct mail	
	Press/journal advertising	
	Radio/TV advertising	
	Poster advertising	END USERS
	Local media advertising/inserts	
	Product literature	
	Leaflets, brochures	
	Leaflet drops	
	Facility visits	
	Exhibitions, symposia, conferences	
	Promotions, competitions	
	After-sales/technical service	
	Complaints handling	
	Gifts	
	Giveaways (funny hats and tee shirts)	INFLUENCERS
	Posters	
	Yellow Pages and other directories	
	Clubs and societies	
	and the list goes on ... and on.	

Which channels will be cost effective for your business?

Promote benefits to the customer

You know what you make. Do you know what your customers buy?
Use this schedule to link the features you expensively build into your product or service to real benefits to your customers.

Your product's features	So what benefit do these features bring to your customer?	Customer benefits	Any further benefits?
Size			
Colour			
Weight			Distil into a 50-word summary your product's promise
Taste			
Feel			
Smell			
Others			

Selling, advertising and promotion should be based on the important customer benefits

Your target market

The target market is the group – or groups – of individuals to whom your business most successfully communicates its key messages in order for you to succeed.

Define your target market by:

- Age
- Sex
- Location
- Social group
- Job title or occupation
- Special interests
- Life style
- Events/features
- Seasonality
- Other important descriptions

   Estimated number of individuals making up target group in your location:

Are there other target markets useful to your business which you can define?

Choosing your advertising medium

Selection of the best advertising medium is for the most part based on the costs of hitting the agreed target market. This table will allow media cost comparisons to be made.

NB. Origination, artwork and production costs must also be assessed.

Where figures are difficult to obtain, some low-cost experimentation will be necessary. Monitoring of results is, of course, even more important than usual.

PRINT	Audited circulation	Researched readership	Target market readership	Cost per 1000 target market	How does this medium relate to your product/service?
Newspapers					
Journals					

BROADCASTING	Audience research	Target market audience	Cost per 1000 target market	How does this medium relate to your product/service?
Radio				
Television				
Cable television				
Cinema				

DIRECT SELLING

	List and delivery research	Target market delivery	Cost per 1000 target market	How does this medium relate to your product/service?
Direct mail				
Leafleting				
Telephone selling				

SHOWS AND EXHIBITIONS

	Attendance	Target market attendance	Cost per 1000 target market	How does this medium relate to your product/service?
Shows				
Exhibitions				
Conferences				

Monitoring of local advertising

Direct response advertising (including coupons) lends itself to ready cost-effectiveness comparisons. This information should be collected for every campaign as a means of improving future campaigns.

This same table may be easily adapted to monitor direct mail and telephone sales campaigns.

Publication						
Frequency*						
Circulation (000s)	(a)					
Number of insertions	(b)					
Cost per insertion £	(c)					
Cost per 000 circulation £	$\frac{c}{a}$					
Cost of campaign £	(d) =	$b \times c$				
Number of enquiries	(e)					
Number of quotations	(f)					
Number of orders	(g)					
Value of orders	(h)					
Cost per enquiry £	$\frac{d}{e}$					
Cost per order £	$\frac{d}{g}$					
Cost per £ order value	$\frac{d}{h}$					

*Quarterly, monthly, weekly or daily

PRESS RELEASE

Macclesfield Business Ventures

Registered Office. Venture House, Cross Street Macclesfield SK11 7PG. Telephone 0625 615113

FREE ADVERTISING THROUGH EDITORIAL

Small businesses are full of news. News about people, products, premises, policies and progress. But surprisingly, the low cost promotional opportunities through news releases are neglected by small business.

To put this right, build a story round people and their success. Keep to the facts. Write the story in short sentences. Summarise the story in the first paragraph. Get the story typed with wide margins, double spaced. Include interesting quotations from key people. Avoid underlining and indiscriminate use of capital letters. Spell numbers one to nine, thereafter use figures. Use eight inch by five inch black and white photographs where possible. But photographs need clear accurate captions attached to them.

Select your target publications to include local, regional and national press, appropriate trade and technical publications, radio and television. Be sure to get your material to them by their copy date.

ENDS ...

Contact:	Name	Phone
	Address	
		Date

Direct mail reduces marketing costs and gains new customers

Macclesfield Business Ventures

Registered Office. Venture House, Cross Street, Macclesfield SK11 7PG. Telephone 0625 615113

Mr J Smith
Managing Director
Buggins Ltd
Industrial Estate
Newtown NW1T 0WN

Dear Mr Smith

Would you like to reduce marketing costs? Would you like new customers?

For small but growing businesses like yours, DIRECT MAIL can be the most cost-effective way of bringing in new business.

Using bought-in mailing lists costing between £50 and £100 per thousand addresses, your message can be accurately delivered to your best prospects for between £200 and £300 per thousand. Using your own existing customer lists may be both cheaper and provide a better response.

These are the main questions for you to consider:

* What is the message to be communicated?
* What action do you want your prospect to take?
* What steps will you take to make it easy for your prospect to reply?
* What plans do you have to follow up non-responders?
* Have you the capacity and staff to handle the replies?
* What response rate are you expecting?
* Is the expense likely to produce a profit benefit?

> Experience in direct marketing by mail shows that mailings which arrive with your prospect on Tuesdays obtain the best response rates. Most successful direct marketers avoid holiday periods and 'silly seasons'.

CAPITALS, underlining, asterisks and postscripts all improve the chances of bringing in the business. Of course, keep it simple. Use short sentences. A personalised greeting, as in this letter, Mr Smith, and a legible signature, also help response rates.

Telephone your marketing adviser NOW to set up a small test campaign.

Your sincerely

A. Seller

A. Seller

PS Did you know that the Post Office have free introductory offers on first mail shots and Business Reply licences? Get the facts from their Sales Office TODAY.

Methods of selling

Even the one-person company must sell hard. From the almost limitless list of sales opportunities, 24 of the most common are reviewed below.

	To the trade	To the public	Comments	Estimate the cost
Personal visit	✓	✓	Gets in the way of other activities	
Salesman	✓	?	Can be difficult to control	
Sales agent	✓	✓	Paid according to results	
Telephone sales	✓	✓	New skill?	
Mailing	✓	✓	Low response rate. Can be targeted	
Poster		✓	Cheap to produce. Costly to post	
Radio	?	✓	Good for special segments of the market	
Television	?	✓	Expensive for small business. NB. Channel 4	
Newspapers	?	✓	Good cover. Wasted readership	

Journals
  Trade and technical
  General interest
  Special interest
	
	✓
	?
	
		?
		✓
		✓
			Response may be measurable	

Leaflets/brochures				
Mail order		✓	Difficult to get into catalogue	

Shows/exhibitions
  Trade
  General
	
	✓
	
		✓
			Sometimes essential. Beware of unprofitable turnover	

Directories	✓	?	Yellow Pages and similar	
Party plan		✓	Beware of pyramid selling	
Cinema	?	✓	Declining audiences. Good for some segments	

	To the trade	To the public	Comments	Estimate the cost
In-store demonstrations		✓	Good visibility – check sales/profits	
Shop window cards	?	✓	Useful for trades/skills of local interest	
Sampling/trial use	✓	?	Expensive. May help an excellent product	
Editorial	✓	✓	Often overlooked – almost free	
Facility visits	✓	?	Visits to premises	
Complaints	✓	✓	Always a new sales opportunity	
Conferences	✓		Useful for specialised technical message	
Competitions/promotions	✓	✓	Can bring life to a dull product	

Exhibitions and shows

Effective participation in a well chosen exhibition can work wonders for a small, little known business seeking new business with individual, small, medium-sized and larger businesses. Common problems include:

- Choosing an unsuitable exhibition
- Underestimating the manpower and costs involved in the exhibition
- Forgetting to brief staff on the purpose of being there
- Omitting to follow up on all interested contacts after the exhibition.

Put simply, exhibitions are either horizontal or vertical.

Horizontal
Appealing to a wide cross section of the population:

Business to Business Exhibition
Royal Show
Ideal Homes Exhibition.

Vertical
Appealing in depth to a specific audience:

Cruft's Dog Show
Congress of Cardiology
Offshore Inspection Repair and Maintenance Exhibition.

What local 　　　regional 　　　national exhibitions meet your business needs?	

What are the costs involved? 　　Space hire 　　Stand design 　　　building 　　　services 　　　fitting 　　Manning costs: people × cost/day 　　Additional print material and gifts 　　Travel, entertainment, accommodation	£ £ £ £ £ £ £ £
Total	£
+ Costs of not doing other priority things	£
What are your objectives? 　　Direct sales off the stand 　　Lead generation 　　Product enquiries 　　Product launch How will follow-up be done?	£ Number: Number:

How many customers?

Answer: Fewer than you might first imagine

Estimated annual sales	£	(a)
Average size of sales transaction	£	(b)
∴ Annual number of sales transactions (a) ÷ (b)		(c)
Average annual frequency of customer purchase		(d)
∴ Annual number of customers* (c) ÷ (d)		(e)
Number of existing customers		(f)
Number of new customers needed (e) – (f)	_____	

* For very small business, this number often lies in the range:

　30 – for special trade selling operations

　to

　300 – for retail shops

BUT harder to obtain than you would ever have thought
Now look at the sales cascade (next page).

The sales cascade

In business start-ups and expansions, it is easy to overlook the workload encountered in generating new business. For example, for every five leads you have, you are only likely to make three relevant contacts. For every three contacts, only 1.5 get to first interview. If you work through the left-hand columns in the grid below, you will see that one order might need an original 101.25 contacts!

The number of interviews varies with the type of product or its market.	Conversion rates from one level to the next		Number required to meet your sales plan	Time/cost involved £ or hours
	Typical	Your business		
Success One order	3		Orders/ customers required ☐	
Third interview Final bid for the business	1.5	☐	Third interviews ☐	
Second interview Handling objections Confirming details	1.5		Second interviews ☐	
First interview The initial sales presentation	3	☐	First interviews ☐	
Contacts Conversation with named, relevant person, often prelude to an appointment	5		Contacts ☐	
Leads An address, phone number, possibly a name. Can you generate enough?			Leads ☐	
Multiplier effect	101.25			

61

Selling to large buyers

Most large organisations, such as ICI, Shell, and local authorities, are keen to encourage the development of new small suppliers. But almost all of them need to be satisfied about the reliability and financial stability of the supplier.

The following form is reproduced from the Cheshire County Council procedure for becoming an approved supplier.

To: CONTROLLER OF SUPPLIES CHESHIRE COUNTY COUNCIL	APPLICATION FOR INCLUSION ON THE COUNTY'S SELECT LIST OF CONTRACTORS
1. Name of applicant (individual or organisation)	To be completed by the applicant
2. Address for normal business	
3. State whether independent, or whether subsidiary or member of group	
4. Turnover in £ sterling in respect of main goods (or services) being offered	
5. Percentage that above represents in relation to the overall turnover	
6. Specialities offered (goods or services)	
7. Extent of technical or other services available to your customers (as applicable). (a) technical, (b) maintenance (c) design	(a) (b) (c)

To: CONTROLLER OF SUPPLIES CHESHIRE COUNTY COUNCIL	APPLICATION FOR INCLUSION ON THE COUNTY'S SELECT LIST OF CONTRACTORS
8. Name other local authorities from whom you have been awarded contracts during past five years (state full addresses)	
9. Other public organisations to whom you are currently supplying goods or services (state full addresses)	(a) (b) (c)
10. Value of such contracts	8(a) 8(b) 8(c) 9(a) 9(b) 9(c)
11. Any other relevant information which will aid the Controller of Supplies in the consideration of your application	

Sales control

To encourage attention to selling, this daily activity report has been drawn up. Even the one-person business can use the report, doing so for those days or part days in the week when active selling is done.

Daily activity report											
					Date						
Customer*	Call type**		New(N) or existing (E) customer	Order size £	Products detailed***						Information****
	C or I	T or V			1	2	3	4	5	6	7	

NO CUSTOMERS - NO BUSINESS

*****

TOTAL C =   TOTAL N =
TOTAL I =   TOTAL E =
TOTAL V =
TOTAL T =

SALES £

FINISH   Miles –
START   Miles –

TOTAL   Miles –

EXPENSES - accommodation
          - meals
          - petrol etc

TOTAL   £

* Name/Town
** Sales call   C
   Sales interview   I
   Telephone interview T
   Visit   V
*** Products by reference number
**** Miscellaneous, eg Order gained from
                       Order lost to
***** Weekly and monthly figures may be carried forward

Control ratios such as:
Orders/Interviews =
Interviews/Calls =
£ Order value/£ Travelling cost =
can be calculated.

Customer control

A customer record should exist for all major customers upon whom regular sales calls are to be made. A specimen is shown below.

Customer record

ACCOUNT

CONTACT

BUSINESS TYPE

PHONE

Best Time/Day/Month

POTENTIAL SALES
£   /year

Date	Payment status*	Objectives**	Results	Order value	Products	Objections***

* Checked prior evening
** Write objectives for next call to this customer immediately after sales call
*** For future interview planning

Channels of distribution

How will your goods reach the end user?

What channels of distribution do your competitors use?

Use this map to identify the best channels for your products to reach the end user.

How do your chosen channels influence your:

- Prices?
- Discounts?
- Advertising?

Forecasting sales

The firm which cannot generate a *sales forecast* has no reason to be in business. Nevertheless sales forecasting is not easy, nor is it always accurate. Here are five ways in which your sales can be predicted. Use one or more methods.

1. Customers × orders

Average size of sales transaction	×	Customers		Sales £
£	×	/day /week /month /year	=	/day /week /month /year

Take seasonal factors into account.

2. Product/customer matrix

Customer	Z	Y	X	W	V	Product totals £
Product						
A						
B						
C						
D						
E						
Customer totals £						Grand Total

NB. In many businesses 80 per cent of sales will come from 20 per cent of products/customers.

Have you asked your customers about their buying plans?

3. Extrapolation of present trends

	Actual				Forecast growth	
Annual sales	1984	1985	1986	1987	1988	1989
Divided by annual sales	÷	÷	÷	÷		
in previous year	1983	1984	1985	1986		
∴ Annual growth =	%	%	%	%	%	%

4. 'Z' charts
The trend of moving annual total sales (= sales in last 12 months) will suggest future levels of sales. Intermediate sales targets can also be set. The example shows seasonal sales to December.

5. Market share

Year	Total market in units (a)	Competitors' market share %					Your company share % (b)	Your sales units (a) × (b)	Your selling price £/unit	Sales forecast £
		A	B	C	D	E				
1985 1986 1987										
1988 1989										

69

Now check:

	£	Units
Sales forecasts		
Production capacity		

The marketing plan for bigger businesses

For larger start-ups and major expansions, a written detailed marketing plan is desirable. Financiers may wish to see it incorporated into your business plan.

The marketing plan is the blueprint for marketing action and the document used for monitoring performance to show whether marketing objectives are being achieved. There are a number of possible formats in common use; this is one variation.

1. **Introduction and background**

   Assessment of market potential: market research information.

   Analysis of Strengths, Weaknesses, Opportunities, Trends: (SWOT analysis).

   Analysis of competitive situation: existing market shares, competition, marketing strategies; possible counter moves, other likely reaction.

   Examination of human resources: key personnel, their responsibilities and potential.

2. **Marketing strategy outline**

   Existing products: are they in growth, maturity, decline?

   Proposed new products: pre-launch/launch planning, investment plans.

   Written statements summarising product attributes: the brand propositions or brand intentions.

   Features/Benefits analysis: key consumer benefits and competitive comparisons – Unique Selling Proposition (USP).

   Proposed pricing strategy: what will the market stand?

   Proposed distribution strategy: manufacturing/warehousing facilities, locations and costs.

3. **Strategic objectives. Where are we going?**

   What targets, benchmarks of achievement do we set ourselves?

   Are these detailed, specific and measurable?

   Are they relevant, clearly understandable, challenging/demanding but achievable?

   Marketing action plans to achieve above objectives, resources required and their deployment.

4. **Marketing monitoring and control**
   Detailed breakdown of action plan (in 3 above) with monitoring methods.

Sales projections		Sales territory	
Profit projections	broken	Product	– 1 year firm
Market shares/penetration	down by	Key market	– 2 years indicative
Selling expense		Major accounts	

   Sales operating budgets detailing each of the above features with
   projected attainment levels for each of the designated accounting/trading
   periods (usually monthly, sometimes quarterly/weekly).

5. **Physical stock levels at key dates**
   To meet seasonal variations permitting steady production with minimum
   inventory levels.

6. **Marketing support activities** needed to achieve the proposed objectives,
   eg:

   Sales training programmes
   Recruitment of additional personnel – job descriptions
   Advertising/sales promotion agency briefs
   Market research briefs etc.

7. **Longer term strategic objectives**
   Research and development
   New product developments
   New market development
   Diversifications etc.

For many projects, the marketing plan is an important component in an
overall business plan.

5
Now I Need the Cash ...

Sources of finance

The sources of finance are basically few in number. The list is properly
headed by: self, family and friends.

1. **Self, family and friends**
   Loans and equity

2. **Shareholders and directors**
   Loans and equity

3. **Internal company sources** (not applicable to start-ups)
   Retained profits, cash collection, stocks and creditors

4. **Clearing banks**
   Overdraft, short-, medium- and long-term loans, Loan Guarantee
   Scheme
   Also some start-up and equity packages
   (Some building societies will provide long-term business development
   loans.)

5. **Second-tier finance**
   Hire purchase, leasing, contract hire, sale and leaseback, factoring and
   invoice discounting (see pages 75–6)

6. **Specialist financial institutions**
   Merchant banks and Investors in Industry Group (now called 3i)
   British Technology Group
   Pension funds
   Investment trusts
   Insurance companies
   Plus: Banks other than clearing banks
         Some local authorities, development corporations and enterprise
         boards

7. **Venture development capital**
   Venture capital funds
   Business Expansion Scheme funds (equity only)
   Private investors

8. **Mergers and acquisitions**

9. **Grants**
   Government and local authorty
   Trusts: Prince's Youth Business Trust, Royal Jubilee, Youth Enterprise
   Scheme

10. **Money lenders**
    Mentioned for the sake of completeness only, and not to be used in
    business.

How much have 'Self, family and friends' provided?   £

What proportion of total start-up funds does this come to?   %

Second-tier finance

Brief descriptions of additional financing options are given below.
Professional advice from your accountant should clarify which, if any, would
suit the business best.

Hire purchase

- Outright ownership of the equipment at the end of the hire period.
- Capital allowances and other grants may be claimed at the outset by the
  hirer.
- Hire purchase usually requires a deposit, and hire payments comprise
  capital and interest – only the interest element is tax deductible.

Lease purchase

- Where no deposit is payable by the hirer, the agreement may be called
  lease purchase.

Leasing (sometimes referred to as tax or finance leases)

- Capital allowances and grants are held by the leasing company, and in
  some measure passed on as reduced rentals.
- At the end of the lease period, a secondary period of lease may be taken
  up as an option at a nominal rental. Alternatively, the equipment may
  be purchased via a third party with drawback to the lessee.
- Lease rentals are treated as expenses, and therefore deductible against
  tax.
- Closed end leases run for a fixed term of one to five years. Open ended
  leases can be terminated at any time after the nominated minimum
  period. Balloon leases allow part of the capital payment to be made at
  the end of the lease agreement.

Contract hire (operating leases)

- Differs from finance leases in that the lessor is responsible for
  maintenance and, if necessary, replacement of the asset. Useful where
  the term of the lease is short when compared to the life of the assets.

Sale and leaseback

- An agreement between the seller and lessor wherein the seller undertakes to take a lease on the equipment, usually properties or large capital asset, for an agreed and long-term period. It releases cash for more profitable investment elsewhere but reduces the security in the business.
- An agreement between a firm and an institution wherein the firm sells its property, or a large item of equipment, to the institution, and at the same time takes out a long-term lease on it for the institution.
- Releases capital for use in the business. Tax aspects need watching.

Summary

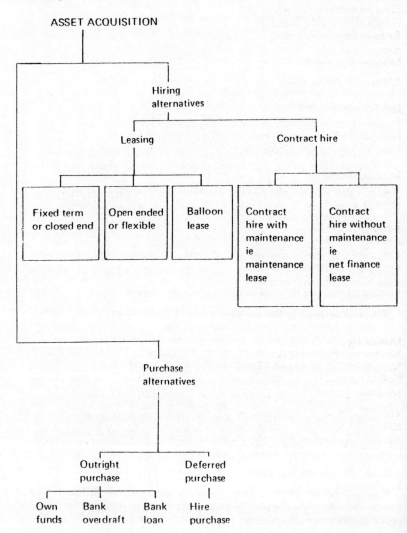

Factoring and invoice discounting

These two similar services may be used to bring a one-off improvement to cash flow.

Factoring

Factoring is selling your business debts to the factoring company on a continuing basis in order to obtain immediate cash payments in place of the expected future payments. The factoring service includes sales ledger, invoicing, insurance, cash collection and credit control systems.

Advantages
Suits growth companies
Avoids extension of overdraft
Reduces administration
Reduces bad debts*
Efficient paperwork

* Non-recourse factoring

Disadvantages
Expensive – usually involves interest and service charges
More difficult for a young business to get accepted
Concern about effect on customers

Invoice discounting

A simple service which makes cash advances against some or all sales invoices.

Advantages
Cheaper than factoring
Customer relations unaffected
Suits growth companies
Avoids extension of overdraft
Reduces bad debts*

* Non-recourse invoice discounting

Disadvantages
Needs well rated invoices
No help with sales administration
Expensive – usually involves interest and service charges
More difficult for a young business to get accepted by the finance house

The Association of British Factors, 24–28 Bloomsbury Way, London WC1A 2PX; telephone 071-831 4268, and the Association of Invoice Factors, 7 North Street, Belfast BT1 1FF; telephone 0232 324522, exist to help their members and to control standards within the industry.

Equipment leasing

For smaller businesses the place of leasing in the mix of financial opportunities is not always clear.

Advantages
Reduces capital need for start-up or expansion
Off balance sheet, therefore leaves balance sheet ratios unaffected
Quick, often easy, to arrange
Stable facility, cannot be withdrawn
'Full service' or flexible leasing options
Tax advantage to sole trader or partnership in first trading period
Useful when equipment with only limited life needed, say three to five years,
    where capital could best be deployed for more long-term use

Disadvantages
Expensive
Restrictions on use of equipment and, for cars, a limit on tax relief
Medium-term inflexible contract
Asset now owned by user
Tax credits, if applicable, taken by lessor

Before completing a lease agreement:

1. Understand nature of proposed agreement.
2. Check term, interest rate, inclusions, exclusions.
3. Note any method of residual valuation and payment.
4. Note trade-in and cancellation penalties.
5. Obtain cash flow and after-tax costs.

Matching finance

Money raised by a business should be matched to the purposes to which it is
to be applied.

*A common error is to use an overdraft facility to purchase plant and equipment; never mix up
long-term and short-term financing.*

This list relates types, sources, and purposes of finance.

Equity funding

Purpose of finance
Core finance
Permanent capital

Sources of equity funding
Self, family, shareholders, and retained profits
Trusts*
Private investors
Development corporations and boards
Venture capital funds
Merchant banks
Insurance companies
Pension funds
Business competitions

Short-term funding (0–3 year money)

Purpose of finance
Short-term working capital needs

- seasonal requirements
- bridging finance

Sources of short-term funding
Self, family, directors' loans and retained profits
Debtors, stock reduction and extension of credit from suppliers
Trusts*
Clearing and other banks (overdraft)
Merchant banks
Finance houses
Leasing companies
Factoring and invoice discounting companies
Money lenders

Medium-term funding (2–10 year money)

Purpose of finance
Medium-term assets
- plant and machinery

Hard core working capital
- research and development

Sources of medium-term funding
Self, family, directors' loans and retained profits
Clearing and other banks (term loan and Loan Guarantee Scheme)
Development corporations and boards
Merchant banks
Finance houses
Leasing companies
Central and local government loans and grants
EEC loans

Long-term funding (10–25 year money)

Purpose of finance
Long-term assets
- land, buildings

Corporate development

Sources of long-term finance
Self, family, directors' loans and retained profits
Clearing and other banks
Some building societies
Development corporations and boards
Merchant banks
Finance houses

Leasing companies
Central and local government loans and grants
EEC loans
Insurance companies
Pension funds

* Several trusts exist to provide money for start-ups, notably for the under
25 age group: Royal Jubilee and Prince's Youth Business Trust, Youth
Enterprise Scheme.

Cash required to start the business

The cash position is calculated in the forecasts for years 1 and 2 (see pages
81–5). Without this calculation, there may be a tendency to underestimate
the cash necessary to start the business.

It will be difficult to raise more than half the cash required to start the
business from external sources, such as the bank.

This diagram shows the way cash flows out of, and later, we hope, back into
a business. Its purpose is to encourage the calculation of the total cash
needed to cover the worst cash position – this often occurs some months
after start-up. When this figure is known, own cash 'o' and external cash 'x'
from, say, the bank, may then be calculated.

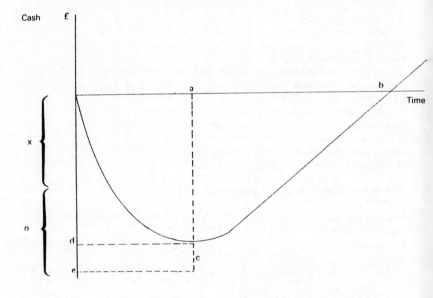

a = Time of worst cash position

b = Time of break-even on cash

c = Contingency – say 10 per cent of d

d = Worst cash position

e = c + d = *cash to start business*

o = Own finance (approximately equal to x)

x = External finance

z = Point at which second phase expansion
may begin, often with a negative cash flow
of its own

Break-even point

As part of the start-up – and as part of the business plan – it is instructive to calculate the sales revenue necessary to break even against total costs.

Sales revenue	=	Units × price
Variable costs	=	Those costs which vary directly with throughput, eg raw materials
Fixed costs	=	Those costs which remain unchanged by throughput, eg rent
Total costs	=	Variable costs + fixed costs

The break-even graph often looks like this:

Now calculate:

$$\frac{\text{Break-even volume}}{\text{Production capacity}} \times 100 = \text{per cent}$$

$$\frac{\text{Break-even volume}}{\text{Current year sales target}} \times 100 = \text{per cent}$$

The higher these percentages, the less able the business is to withstand business uncertainty. Rethink when percentages exceed 70 per cent

$$\text{Gross margin \%} = \frac{\text{Sales revenue} - \text{variable cost}}{\text{Sales revenue}} \times 100$$

$$\text{Sales to break even} = \frac{\text{Fixed cost}}{\text{Gross margin}} \times 100$$

$$\text{Profit} = (\text{Sales revenue} - \text{sales to break even}) \times \frac{\text{Gross margin}}{100} \, (\%)$$

The business plan

In an ideal world, the case presented to outside financial institutions should comprise the following. The proprietors also invest in the business; they too should have this information available.

1. *History of the business*
   A brief summary of the trading record and activities of the business since its inception, or during the last five years, whichever is the shorter. This paragraph would also include the numbers of employees through the period. List registered office, bankers, auditors/accountant, solicitor, and company registration numbers.

2. *Shareholders and senior managers*
   Include the major shareholders and their stakes. Describe the career details of the senior managers focusing on their successful track record throughout their careers.

3. *The market-place*
   Describe the market-place by, for example, geography, customers, business sector. Identify where possible total market potential, current existing market, and your target share of market.

   Examine major competitors in the major markets identified paying particular attention to their pricing and product improvement performance.

   Show the sales, marketing and distribution methods in use for the major parts of the business.

4. *Products and/or services*
   Describe the current range of products and services offered by the business, identifying the unique features and selling benefits associated with each one. Comment on the potential for *adding value* to existing products and services, and for developing totally new products and services.

5. *Business strategy (the five-year dream)*
   Write brief summary paragraphs that describe the overall business strategy, and the major functions of the business. These are likely to include capital structuring and financing, development, manufacturing, distribution, marketing, relationships with suppliers, premises, equipment. Note also the future management structure.

6. *Shorter-term objectives*
   A brief list of the major problems and opportunities that the management intend to face and to take up during the forthcoming 12 months.

   This paragraph should include the major assumptions made about conditions which will affect the business.

7. *Management information system*

A short demonstration of how major functions of the business are positively controlled by the existing management. Examples include credit control, research and development, cost control, purchase control, production cost control, cash flow control, sales control.

8. *Financial requirements*

Tabular information designed to analyse the future financial requirements including the timing of intended expenditures, their sizes, the purpose of the expenditure and its planned benefit to the business.

For larger projects, break-even levels of sales and sensitivity analyses would be helpful. (Computer packages used by professional accountants can produce these simply and effectively.) Include the contributions to the future cash requirements to be made by the shareholders and other sources of capital. Describe the repayment plans.

9. *Basic financial information*

This should include the audited accounts for up to five years and the interim figures, ideally on a quarterly basis, for the current financial year. This should enable an up-to-date forecast for the current financial year to be made.

For future periods, information should be presented to cover the operating budget and hence the cash flows for the next 12 months analysed at least by quarterly, and preferably by monthly, intervals. Outline budgets and cash flows for the following two years would also be most helpful. Summarise this information in the profit and loss accounts and balance sheets.

10. *Security*

As a reserve document, not for immediate presentation, it is desirable to have available a summary of opportunities to provide personal security, business security, and the status of directors' loans.

Also have available the Memorandum and Articles of Association, and Partnership Agreements, where applicable. Prepare for a visit by the financier to the premises.

Business forecasts

To help your accountant in the preparation of forecast cash flows, profit and loss accounts and balance sheets for the next three years, this basic data should be collected.

Business forecasts

VAT status

VAT rate	%
VAT pay date	

Financing

	Equipment (if applicable)		Deposit	
	Item	Cash cost £	Date payable	Size £
Loan • • •				
Hire purchase • • •				
Leasing • • •				

Operating statistics

			Year 1	Year 2	Year 3
Stock cover at year end					
raw materials	days				
work in progress	days				
finished goods	days				
Gross margin	%				

	Pre start-up or last financial year end
Receipts	
Proprietors'/shareholders' capital introduced	
Directors'/shareholders' loans	
Grants/other	

Payments

Fixtures/fittings
Equipment

Note. Enter description and *either* amount paid when bought outright, *or* complete financing

gistration	Not required/Voluntary/Compulsory*
dustry	Exempt/Zero rated/Mixed/Fully rated*
	* Delete as applicable

Advance		Repayments				Interest rate
te	Size £	Date of first	Frequency	Size £	Term months	% APR

Current overdraft facility

£ _____

			Year 1	Year 2	Year 3
Average time to collect debts	days				
Average time to pay suppliers	days				
Materials/sales	%				
Direct labour/sales	%				
Cash sales/total sales	%				

Months											Year 1 Total	Quarters				Year 2 Total	Year 3 Total
2	3	4	5	6	7	8	9	10	11	12		1	2	3	4		

above.

83

Now complete as much as possible of this form. With the exception of financing costs, write the figures on the basis of sales made and costs incurred (not as paid) and *exclusive of VAT*.

	Pre start up or last financial year end
Sales	
Direct materials	
Year end stock*	
Usage	
Purchases pattern	
NB. Total purchases for year = Closing stock + Usage – Opening stock. Purchases per period = Total purchases for the year spread according to purchase pattern.	
Direct labour (inc NI)	
Selling and distribution	
Carriage	
Packing	
Advertising and promotion	
Travel	
Sales salaries (inc NI)	
Sales commissions	
Others	
Occupation and administration	
Rent	
Rates	
Post	
Gas**	
Electricity**	
Water**	
Printing and stationery	
Insurances	
Repairs and maintenance	
Decoration and minor improvements	
Telephone***	
Professional fees	
Bank charges	
Salaries (inc NI)	
Others	
Financing costs (likely to be computed by your accountant)	
Overdraft interest	
Loan interest	
Hire purchase/leasing charges	

* Pre start-up or last year end figures only
** Include connection charges
*** Include connection, equipment, rentals and call costs.

Months												Year 1 Total	Quarters				Year 2 Total	Year 3 Total
1	2	3	4	5	6	7	8	9	10	11	12		1	2	3	4		

Basic rules of bank lending

The clearing banks operate to simple lending rules. The business plan will recognise the rules and adapt to them.

1. **Equal contributions from the businessman and the bank**
   - the '£ for £' rule, *or*
   - shareholders'/proprietors' equity: borrowing = 1:1

2. **Full security on the bank's lending**
   Often provided by:
   - personal guarantees
   - land (including buildings)
   - stocks and shares
   - life assurance policies
   - business assets, eg debtors, stock, fixed assets.

   The bank requires the security to be easy to value, readily marketable and easy to obtain good legal title to.

   NB. The Loan Guarantee Scheme (LGS) now operates for some cases for which available security is insufficient to support the required loan, see opposite page.

3. **Capacity to service interest charges**
   The degree to which planned profits exceed interest charges varies from bank to bank, but aim at a multiple of 4:1.

4. **Capability to repay the loan**
   The ability to repay within the term.

   The business plan will cover paragraphs 1 to 4 above and describe the nature of the proposition.

Finally, and probably most important:

5. **The borrower himself**
   - his integrity and reliability
   - his capability of carrying out his business plan.

Presenting your case personally to the bank

The bank manager is required to make an assessment of you and your project. While the business plan will say much about the project, the presentation interview will be the best time to communicate your enthusiasm, commitment, and ability to manage. Use this 10 point checklist:

1. Complete the business plan. Include details according to the size of the finance package required.

2. Identify a 'preferred' list of bank branches with named managers, your own bank to head the list.

3. Personalise the front page and the summary of the plan to each of the 'preferred' list bank managers.

4. Make an appointment of a sensible duration with a manager of appropriate seniority, having regard to the size of the financial package requested.

5. Leave the business plan with the manager three to four days ahead of the appointment.

6. Plan out the main points you wish to stress during your introductory comments at the interview.

7. Arrive early for the appointment, appropriately dressed.

8. Make main points simply and quickly, and in so doing show how well you understand the market for your product or service.

9. Answer the manager's questions to amplify and support the written business plan in a way which will demonstrate your personal capability to run the business and your commitment to it.

10. Ask for the finance specified on front page (3 above).

The bank manager then has three responses:

Responses	Your reaction
1. Agree	Ask about costs, interest rate and conditions, obtain facility letter.
2. Want to think about it	Agree decision date, submit any further needed information.
3. Reject	Find out objections and try to agree a re-presentation date.

The government-backed Loan Guarantee Scheme (LGS)

In the absence of sufficient security, the major banks may use the LGS to help business start-ups and expansions. The money is expensive with a 5 per cent premium on the guaranteed element of the loan, but it can overcome some of the basic rules of bank lending (see page 85). See how it might work in the following small start-up. Then write in your own figures.

Typical start-up

	(% of sales)	First year of trade £000	Your forecasts for first year
Sales		20	[ ]
Gross margin	(50%)	10	[ ]
Profit (pre-tax, pre-interest, loan)	(10%)	2	[ ]
Fixed assets		5	[ ]
Equipment	4		
Vehicles	1		
Stock and debtors	(40%)*	8	[ ]
Creditors	(13%)*	3	[ ]

* See *The Genghis Khan Guide to Business*, Brian Warnes (Osmosis Publications Ltd)

Two financing options
(examples only)

(a) Proprietor/Shareholders alone	£000	(b) Using Loan Guarantee Scheme (LGS)	£000	
Investment, say	10	Overdraft @ 14% (secured)	5.0	
		3-year guaranteed loan @ 16%	5.0	
		∴ Overdraft interest	0.7	
		Loan interest	0.7	
		Loan premium	0.2	
		Charge to P&L	1.6	
Profit (pre-tax)	2	Profit (pre-tax)	0.4	
		From which loan repayments of have to be made	1.4	

NB. Proprietor's capital is cheap money.
  LGS does not cover overdraft finance.
  Interest and loan repayments can eliminate profits.
  Business failure rates under LGS are said to be 40 per cent.
  Take advantage of monitoring and reporting required by the lender.

Benefiting from government grants

Many grant aid programmes come under the general description of 'selective financial assistance' which, in turn, covers the Department of Trade and Industry's 'Support for Innovation' and 'Selective Assistance to Manufacturing Industry' packages.

While separate application forms tend to be applicable to each scheme, the following principles apply:

1. The company

(a) Must be viable (but not too viable)
(b) Must be well managed
(c) Should be likely to succeed
(d) Should contact Department of Trade and Industry. Try to get to know personally the officer responsible for the appraisal.

2. The project

(a) Must be viable
(b) Must have a clear end product
(c) Must be additional in that one of the following apply:

- without aid the project would be cancelled
- with aid, the project would be changed beneficially
- its time-scale would be accelerated
- it would be enlarged

(d) Should provide industrial and economic benefits
(e) Must be innovatory, for 'Support for Innovation'
(f) Must be approved *before any expenditure* is incurred.

NB. The approval process itself can also take several months, so there is a need to plan ahead if advantage is to be taken of government grant aid.

Regional Development Grants are available in certain localities. Details should be obtained from the Department of Trade and Industry, Training and Enterprise Councils, or the Local Enterprise Agency.

Schemes and services available to small businesses

Local Enterprise Agencies, Training and Enterprise Councils, and accountants have more detailed information on schemes to benefit your business. The following selection will show where you may be able to find help.

Start-up
Enterprise Allowance Scheme
Training and Enterprise Councils
Local Enterprise Agency
In rural areas of England: Rural Development Commission
In rural areas of Scotland and Wales: Local Development Boards

Up to 200 employees
Training and Enterprise Councils
Local Enterprise Agency
Products and process consultancy
Major project grants
Export Initiative: advice, market entry help, projects grants
Export Credits Guarantee
Training consultancy
Youth Training
In rural areas of England: Rural Development Commission
In rural areas of Scotland and Wales: Local Development Boards

Up to 500 employees
Products and process consultancy
Support for Innovation
Major project grants
Loan Guarantee Scheme
Export Initiative: advice, market entry help, projects grants
Youth Training

For businesses regardless of size (but there may be exempt classes)
Business Expansion Scheme
Support for Innovation
Loan Guarantee Scheme
Local Authority grants and finance
In assisted areas: Regional Selective Assistance
In development areas: Regional Development Grants
In closure areas: EEC, BSC and NCB schemes

Business information document

The Prevention of Fraud Act places the entrepreneur at risk of heavy damages when the public is canvassed for money other than by licensed dealers in securities, eg banks and brokers. The activities and authorisation of investment businesses are now governed by the Financial Services Act 1986. When the time comes to seek additional investment in the business, summary information of the sort indicated below will determine the level of interest in the investor's side. An interested investor would subsequently expect a full business plan. It is important to seek professional advice before canvassing for finance. The rules are strict and must be observed.

Main activities

Main markets and competition

Product range

- Existing products
- New products
- Patent position

Management team

Number of employees

- Past
- Present
- Projected

Main shareholders

(See table opposite.)

		Actual				Proposed		
		1987	1988	1989	1990	1991	1992	1993
Sales	£000							
Gross profit	£000							
Pre-tax profit	£000							
Balance sheet summary								
Issued capital								
Reserves								
Loans (with terms and security)								
Fixed assets								
Investments								
Current assets								
Current liabilities								
Cash requirements								
Capital expenditure								

6

... and Premises

Working from home

Home may be a most suitable first base for the starter business. Whether it is legal and practical is a matter of fact and degree – this checklist may prevent expensive mistakes.

Issue	Check with
Planning permission Building regulations	Planning Department Local Authority

Restrictive covenants
    ● Leasehold
    ● Freehold
	Lease agreement or Title deed
	Solicitor

Mortgage	Building society
Insurance	Insurance company
Tax consequences	Accountant
Other legislation relevant to your business plans	Local Authority Solicitor
Disturbance	Neighbours
Effect on family life and social life	Family
Your own work efficiency at home	Self

If work at home is not practicable or excessive business use might lend to a liability for business rate, it may be worth contacting your Borough, District or County Council, or your Local Enterprise Agency, about managed workshops or nursery units. Such premises are specially designed for start-ups and young businesses.

Property requirements checklist

Before beginning the search, complete the 'Ideal' column describing the property really needed to see the business through its early years. Fill in notes for interesting properties seen. Try to find at least three properties which come near to meeting the ideal needs.

	Ideal	Property A	Property B	Property C
Type				
Warehouse				
Factory				
Office				
Shop				
Location/Town				
How Large? (in sq ft/metres)				
Warehouse				
Factory				
Office				
Shop				
Access				
Pedestrian				
Vehicles				
Loading				
Floor loading				
Height				
Access doors				
Storage space				
Working space				
Parking				
Essential				
Preferable				
Not important				
Facilities				
Office accommodation				
Heating				
Lighting				
Ventilation				
Mains services				
– gas				
– electricity				
– water				
– drainage				
– finishes/insulation				
– security				
– lift				
When available				
Costs				
Purchase				
Rent – Length of lease				
– Annual rent				
– Rent review				
– Premium				

	Ideal	Property A	Property B	Property C
Rateable value				
Legal (Vendor's costs)				
Adaptation and moving costs				
Constraints				
Fire hazards				
Planning permission				
Security				
Refurbishing				
Restrictive covenants				
Future expansion				
Neighbours				
Check also the following points:				
Noise				
Vibration				
Smells				
Overshadowing by buildings, trees etc.				

Rent reviews

Rent reviews have become a fundamental aspect of nearly every modern lease on commercial and industrial property. Landlords are reluctant to grant leases with the rent fixed for a long period, and tenants, notwithstanding their statutory protection, are reluctant to forgo their security by accepting short leases.

The complexities which normally prevail clearly require the experience and skills of professional advisers (see chart opposite).

Lease renewals

In many cases, the expiration of a lease can have an effect similar to that of a rent review, in that the tenant may have been paying an historic rent, in which case the landlord will not have been receiving an economic return on his investment.

Upon the expiry of a lease the contractual commitment by both parties terminates, although the tenant usually has security of tenure under the provisions of the Landlord and Tenant Act 1954, supplemented by the Law of Property Act 1969; thus the relationship between the landlord and tenant will normally continue although the landlord may wish to exercise his statutory right to regain possession of the premises for the purpose of redevelopment of his own occupation, or one of the other statutory reasons.

The highly simplified chart on page 96 describes the process of renewals.

Whether one is landlord or tenant, it is essential to take professional advice at the earliest possible moment.

LANDLORD'S INSTRUCTIONS TO HIS SURVEYOR

Landlord's surveyor serves notice to review the rent in accordance (where appropriate) with the terms of the lease, having carried out an inspection. Counter notice or objection must be served if required by lease. Time limits are strict. Legal advice is essential.

Tenant's instructions to his surveyor and solicitor.

Surveyor liaises with tenant's solicitor then inspects the property. Investigation of lease terms. Measurement of premises. Collection and collation of comparable evidence. Surveyor's advice on rental value and lease terms.

Surveyor negotiates the rent with the other party.

If the tenant rejects proposed rent and there is an irreconcilable disagreement the lease will provide for either an independent expert or arbitrator to be appointed.

Tenant accepts rent.

Appointment of an independent surveyor to act as an expert.

Appointment of arbitrator

Expert invites written representations from each party's surveyor.

Arbitrator gives directions for conduct or arbitration either by written representation or hearing.

Hearing. Surveyor gives evidence in connection with valuation and is cross-examined thereon by counsel for other party.

Each party's surveyor prepares valuation with supporting evidence set out in *proof of evidence*.

If written submission – *points of reply* to other party's case are prepared.

New rental

Tenant has to accept

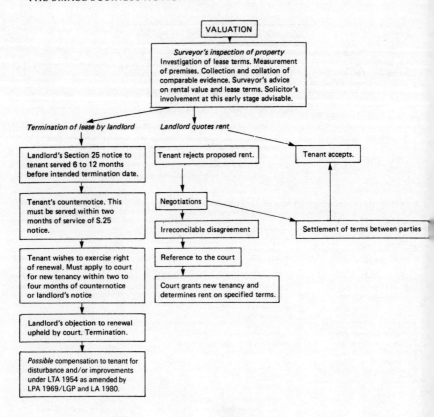

The costs of getting into premises

Most attention is given to rent and rates.

1st year costs

Rent: size	[___ ft²]	×	price	[£ ___ /ft²]	£	
Rates: poundage	[£ ___ /£]	×	rateable value	[£ ___]	£	

TOTAL   £ _____

But the total cost of getting into premises is *increased* by most of the factors listed below:

Other costs	Notes	Amount £
Advance rent	Often three months' rent	
Lease premium	Ask about reverse premium in a slack market	
Survey	Vital for full repairing lease	
Legal	Usually both landlord's and tenant's costs	
Insurances	See lease	
Property improvements	Some may be paid by landlord	
Property alterations	Permission required	
Planning permission	'Change of use' fees	
Services and service charges	3-phase electricity, gas, telephone, ventilation, caretaker, common areas. Who pays? How much?	
Security	Who provides? Who pays?	
Removal	Per quotation	
Disturbance to business	Usually underestimated	
Fire Environmental health and Safety costs	} Check with relevant authorities	
May be aided by		
Moving-in package	Could include rent holiday, legal fees, improvements	

The routine of planning permission

Professional advice will be necessary to help you unravel the intricacies of planning permission. This flowchart has been designed as a much simplified pattern of planning permission routine.

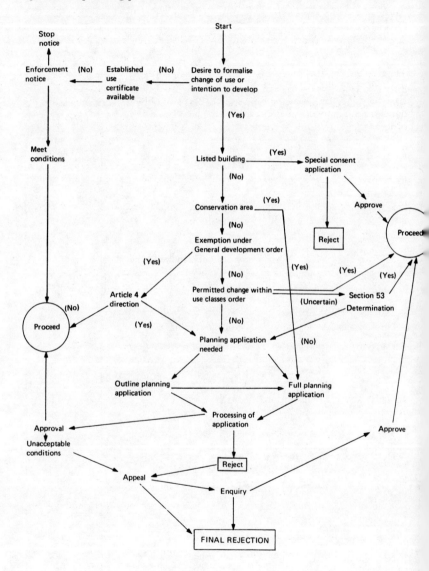

Watch out for opportunities in Special Planning Zones. See *Lifting the Burden on Business*, HMSO, 1985.

A guide to planning applications for commerce and industry

Applications, with appropriate fees, should be made to the Chief Planning Officer, Borough or District Council, for permission to develop land. Applications are needed for new buildings and the change of use of existing buildings or other land.

The checklists below give a quick guide to the information which will generally be required, as a minimum, as part of the planning application. Basically there are two types of planning application, both of which are best done under professional guidance and should be discussed informally with an officer from the Planning Department *before* an application is made.

A. Outline application
An outline application can only be made for the erection of new buildings (or extensions to existing buildings). This will probably be appropriate in cases where it is initially necessary or advisable to establish the *principle* of new industrial development. This will be on land *not* in an industrial area or *not* allocated for industrial use in the local district plans.

An outline application needs:

1. Four completed copies of forms P1 and P1A.
2. Four paper copies of a plan (preferably to a 1:2500 or 1:1250 scale) indicating the land in question within a red edge and any other land owned or controlled edged blue.
3. Any explanatory material which the applicant may wish to give, or which the local planning authority may require.

An outline permission granted will require the submission of a further application (a reserved matters application) giving full details of the new development.

B. Full (detailed) application
A detailed application needs:

1. Four completed copies of forms P1 and P1A.
2. Four paper copies of plans showing:

   (a) The area of land in question within a red edge.
   (b) Plans and elevations of the proposed building(s), including details of materials and finishes.
   (c) Details of the treatment of the remainder of the site, including size, location and surfacing of:

      (i) car parking areas
      (ii) loading, unloading and manoeuvring space
      (iii) open storage space (if any) and details of any proposed screening.

   (d) Details of existing trees together with a proposed landscaping scheme.

Applications will also probably be required under the Building Regulations and an officer in the Planning Department will be pleased to provide advice on this aspect.

Local district or borough plans are available from the Chief Planning Officer, at the council offices.

Change of use: Is planning permission necessary?

The Town and Country Planning (Use Classes) Order 1987 sets out use classes which cover the use of land and buildings. Changes of use which do not require planning permission are set out in Schedule 1 to the General Development Order 1977 as follows:

(a) From Class A3 (food and drink) or from a use for the sale or display for sale of motor vehicles to Class A1 (shops); and

(b) where the total floorspace does not exceed 235 square metres:

(i) From B2 (general industrial) or B8 (storage and distribution) to Class B1 (business)

(ii) From Class B1 (business) or B2 (general industrial) to B8 (storage and distribution).

The Use Classes Order defines a number of terms including 'shop', 'office', 'industrial building', 'light industrial building' and 'general industrial building'. The specified classes should not be stretched to include activities which do not clearly fall within them; unusual activities must be considered as separate uses in themselves. Changes of use to and from any such individual uses will generally require planning permission.

If you are in any doubt about the use class into which your activity falls, or whether planning permission is required for your use of a particular site or building, contact the Borough or District Council Planning Department which will be pleased to advise you.

Categories of use classes

Class

1. Shop, except for sale of

(i) goods other than hot food

(ii) tickets or as a travel agency

(iii) sandwiches or other cold food for consumption off the premises or:

(iv) as a post office

(v) for hairdressing

(vi) for the direction of funerals

(vii) for the display of goods for sale

(viii) for the hiring out of domestic or personal goods or articles

(ix) for the reception of goods to be washed, cleaned or repaired, where the sale, display or service is to visiting members of the public.

2. Use as an office for any purpose

3. Use as a light industrial building for any purpose

4. Use as a general industrial building for any purpose
5. (Special Industrial Group A). Alkali & Works Regulation Act 1906(a), which is not included in any of Classes 6, 7, 8 or 9
6. (Special Industrial Group B). Processes, carried on in or adjacent to a quarry or mine
7. (Special Industrial Group C). Processes based on the treatment of mineral except as an ancillary to the extraction itself
8. (Special Industrial Group D). Use for any of the following purposes:

   (i) oils
   (ii) cellulose
   (iii) linseed oil
   (iv) hot pitch or bitumen
   (v) stoving
   (vi) production contains organic chemicals
   (vii) rubber from scrap
   (viii) chlorphenols or chlorcresols
   (ix) acetylene
   (x) methyl, ethyl amine or acrylates

9. (Special Industrial Group E). Listed industries, businesses or trades
10. Wholesale warehouse or repository for any other purpose
11. Boarding or guest house, or an hotel
12. A residential boarding school, college or training centre
13. Public worship or religious instruction
14. Non-residential educational establishment
15. Health centre, a school treatment centre, a clinic, a crèche, a day nursery or a dispensary, consulting room or surgery
16. Art gallery, a museum, public library or reading room, public hall, exhibition hall
17. Theatre, cinema, music hall or concert hall
18. Dance hall, skating rink, swimming bath, Turkish or foam bath, gymnasium or sports hall.

7

Legal and Tax Matters

Legal format at start-up

The common view is that the 'sole trader' formula is preferable at lower levels of taxable profits. But there is no 'right' answer, and the decision ought to be made on the basis of what best meets the current and foreseeable business needs. Your solicitor or your accountant can help you to make the decision.

Sole trader

Advantages
No legal formalities
Total responsibility
Short-term tax benefits
Taxed as individual
Financial flexibility
May start at any time
Ease of winding up
Self-employed pension facility

Disadvantages
Personal assets at disposal of creditors
Stamp duties when you incorporate
No corporate pension provision
Loss of some social security benefits
Capital Gains Tax on goodwill when you incorporate – subject to deferment

Partnership
As for sole trader plus:

Advantages
Single tax assessment

Disadvantages
Partnership agreement advisable
Difficult to grow through gaining new partners
Each partner responsible for all debts

Limited companies

Advantages
Limited liability*
Lower tax burden at higher profit levels
Company tax burden at higher profit levels
Company pension schemes
Status/Image
May be easier to sell shares depending on initial structure
Loans and shareholders easily added to corporate structure
Employee status for social security benefits

* May be negated in practice by guarantees

Disadvantages
More costly to run
Trading allowed only after incorporation
Loss of profit sharing flexibility
Formal company meetings
Filing of audited accounts
Higher professional fees
Restricted loans to directors
Schedule E taxation for directors
All employees on PAYE
Corporation Tax liability

Co-operative
Owned and controlled by those working in it
- membership usually open to all employees subject to qualifications laid down by the members.
- one member, one vote irrespective of individual shareholdings.

Profits shared in proportion to work, therefore no capital gain.
Members can organise business to suit their own objectives, rather than those of an owner or boss.
Usually registered as either an Industrial and Provident Society or company limited by guarantee.

INDUSTRIAL AND PROVIDENT SOCIETY

Advantages
Model rules for ease of registration
Simpler rules and reporting requirements than companies
Shares easily repurchased by society when a member leaves
Bonus on profits and loan interest paid without deduction of tax
Special Corporation Tax rate
Registrar will advise individual societies
Tax relief on loans used for investing in society
Company pension scheme
Exemption from 'close company' provisions
No directors: management committee elected by members
Organised for the benefit of members who work in the business
No filing fee for annual return

Disadvantages
Shareholding limited to £10,000 per member
Difficult to attract outside risk capital
Share value remains at £1 each
Formal company meetings
Filing of audited accounts
All employees on PAYE
Corporation Tax liability
Minimum of seven members
Not universally understood by accountants, solicitors and bank managers
Not eligible for Business Expansion Scheme funds
Cannot issue bonus shares free of tax
Limited interest only paid on shares
Higher registration cost than company

COMPANY LIMITED BY GUARANTEE
(Not really possible for small business)

Advantages
Model rules for ease of registration
Can be formed with only two members
Easy to join, easy to leave
Company pension scheme
Registered under Companies Act and widely understood by accountants,
    solicitors etc
Possible to obtain charitable status
Constitution may be drafted with more flexibility
Tax relief on loans for investing in company
Organised for benefit of members who work in the business

Disadvantages
No share capital
Difficult to attract outside risk capital
Formal company meetings
Filing of audited accounts
All employees on PAYE
Not eligible for Business Expansion Scheme funds

Note. Can sometimes be registered as a limited company with shares, but
rules are often complex.

Partnerships

Unfortunately, a number of business partnerships have difficulties due to the
absence of a formal partnership agreement.

A partnership agreement drawn up with your accountant's and solicitor's
help before the business begins should consider:

1. Members of the partnership
2. Period of the partnership: commencement, duration and termination
3. Name of the partnership
4. Business activities and location

5. Partnership premises including tenancy agreements/leases
6. Capital: sharing and interest thereon
7. Goodwill
8. Profit (and loss) sharing formula
9. Drawings on account of share of profits
10. Treatment of remuneration, eg partners' fees and legacies from clients of the firm
11. Books of account
12. Annual accounts including accounting date
13. Clients' monies, if applicable
14. Accountants
15. Bankers
16. Responsibilities of partners including holiday entitlement
17. Negative covenants
18. Motor cars
19. Outgoing partners' arrangements
20. Compulsory retirement at given age
21. Admission of new partners
22. Pensions, annuities and insurance arrangements
23. Tax provisions and continuation election
24. Covenants in restraint of trade
25. Dissolution of partnership
26. Expulsion of partners
27. Serving of notices
28. Partnership meetings and voting thereat
29. Arbitration.

Business names

The name a business uses can be a great help to the business but there are a few constraints on the freedom of choice.

Sole trader

1. The individual's own name brings no extra requirements, eg Smith, J Smith.
2. A different name requires:

   - Registration through the Registrar of Companies
   - Letterheads, orders, invoices, receipts, payment demands to bear name and address of owner
   - A notice of the name and address to be prominently displayed in all business premises
   - An answer, in writing, to any request for owner's name and address.

Partnership
As above, except for partnerships of more than 20 persons for which additional regulations apply.

Limited companies
Subject to the approval of the Registrar of Companies, with requirements to avoid:

- The same name as another company
- Criminal, offensive or misleading names
- Names used by certain qualifying entities (eg bank)
- Names connected with the government or royalty, or implying national or international pre-eminence.

There is also a statutory list of words for the use of which prior approval must be obtained.

Formation of limited companies

For some people it may be desirable to form a limited company at the time of start-up. For others, successful expansion may prompt professional advisers to suggest incorporation (formation of a limited company).

1. Memorandum of Association sets out:

(a) Company name
(b) Whether the registered office is in England, Wales, Scotland or Northern Ireland
(c) The company's objects
(d) A statement of the shareholders' liability
(e) The number of authorised shares by type.

2. Articles of Association typically set out:

(a) The procedure for calling general and extraordinary meetings
(b) The responsibilities and rights of directors
(c) Procedure for election of directors
(d) The company's borrowing policies
(e) Control of shares.

A set of model Articles is usually available from accountants and solicitors incorporating the various provisions required by the Companies Acts.

3. Declaration of Compliance on Form G12
States that the directors have complied with Companies Acts.

Your solicitor and accountant will help you with:

Accounting reference date	Form 224
Share allotment	Form 88(2)
Statement of first directors and secretary and intended situation of registered office	Form 10
Statement of change of directors or secretaries	Form 288
Notification of change of registered office	Form 287

Following the submission of these documents by your accountant or solicitor to the Registrar of Companies, and his acceptance, the Certificate of Incorporation will be issued. The Certificate and registration date should be displayed on public view, while the registration number and other formal details must appear on official company stationery.

Responsibilities of company directors

Many people see the position of being a company director as a status symbol. The responsibilities of being a company director, some of which are given below, should encourage you to discuss your individual case with your solicitor or accountant.

- Directors have to attend board meetings.
- They have to disclose their private interests and shares in the company.
- Directors must act with diligence and honesty, and know what is going on.
- They are liable for all debts of the company if, knowing it is insolvent, they allow the company to trade into further debt.

Furthermore, there are these constraints on company directors:

- By the Articles of Association, directors are granted powers which may not be exceeded.
- They are elected and may be removed.
- They are subject to special requirements by the Inland Revenue with regard to expenses and perquisites.
- Normally, directors may not borrow money from the company in excess of £5000.

Value added tax (VAT)

VAT is collected by HM Customs & Excise. Most businesses have to learn to live with it.

1. *Reasons for registering*
   Compulsory when turnover reaches or is likely to reach the VAT threshold.
   High input VAT paid, which is recoverable.
   Credibility with other traders.
   NB. VAT registered customers can claim back invoiced VAT.

2. *Method of registering*
   Discuss with your accountant first.
   Identify VAT trade classification from VAT41 booklet.
   Read 'The VAT Guide' (ref 700).
   Fill in form VAT 1. Send to local VAT office.
   Telephone VAT office for your number.
   Obtain any special leaflets relating to your industry.

3. *Operating the scheme*
   Read 'The VAT Guide' (ref 700).
   Maintain up-to-date, accurate books – see your accountant.
   Prepare to be inspected by an officer of HM Customs & Excise.
   Include VAT payments/receipts in cash flow projections.
   Keep all invoices as evidence of VAT payments.

4. *Remember*
   VAT on bad debts is recoverable only on two-year-old debts written off in your accounts.

VAT is not charged on second-hand car sales except when the car is sold for more than you paid for it.

HM Customs & Excise have available a comprehensive VAT Information Pack; contact your local office.

VAT groups and thresholds
This table enables areas of possible VAT liabilities to be reviewed.

Group	Exempt goods and services A	Zero-rated goods and services B
1.	Land	Food
2.	Insurance	Sewerage and water
3.	Postal services	Books etc
4.	Betting, gaming and lotteries	Books, radio for the handicapped
5.	Finance	News services
6.	Education	Fuel and power
7.	Health	Certain types of construction
8.	Burial and cremation	Protected buildings
9.	Professional bodies and trade unions	International services Transport
10.	Sporting competitions	Caravans, houseboats
11.	Works of art etc	
12.		Gold
13.		Bank notes
14.		Medicines and appliances
15.		Exports, imports
16.		Charities
17.		Children's clothing and footwear

All goods and services not in columns A and B for VAT registered businesses attract VAT at the standard 17.5 per cent rate.

VAT is compulsory when turnover from zero-rated and standard rated goods and services exceeds or is likely to exceed the currently prescribed annual limit. The calculation is based on the past 12 months' turnover and the small business must review turnover monthly and register for VAT if at the end of any month the value of taxable supplies in the last 12 months exceeds the limit, or there are reasonable grounds to believe it will exceed the limit in the next 30 days. Registration takes effect from the end of the month in which the 30 days fall, or such earlier date as may be mutually agreed.

HM Customs & Excise are usually most helpful when queries and uncertainties are put to them.

Tax and the newly self-employed

The tax that you pay for the first *three* tax years that you are in business is normally based on the profits of your *first year alone*. Therefore, with careful planning, you may be able to minimise your tax bills in your early years to your considerable advantage. It is important that you discuss with your accountant as soon as possible how this is best achieved.

At the same time, your accountant should advise you on the best date to which your annual accounts should be prepared so as to delay your tax payments as much as possible, thus maximising your cash flow.

As an *employee*, your income tax and National Insurance contributions were deducted from your remuneration before you received it: that is, you could spend what you received. Now that you are self-employed, your annual income tax and Class 4 National Insurance contributions will normally be payable in two halves: the first half on 1 January in the tax year, and the second half six months later, on 1 July.

Furthermore, your income tax and Class 4 National Insurance bills for the first two or even three tax years are likely to land in your lap together when you least expect them, with only a few days before payment has to be made. You must therefore find out from your accountant what your liabilities are likely to be, and when you might have to pay them.

- It is essential that your cash forecast takes account of your income tax and National Insurance payments so that the cash is there when needed.

Licences and permissions

A wide variety of laws and regulations control and limit certain types of businesses. An indication of licences in which you could be involved follows:

Legislation	*Covering*	
Consumer Credit Act 1974	Credit sales Dealing in securities	
Transport Act 1983	Operators' licences	
Medicines Act 1968	Human and veterinary medicines	
Solicitors' Act 1974		
Veterinary Surgeons Act 1966 and similar Acts	Practice in certain professions	Professional advice from your solicitor is recommended
Registered Homes Act 1984	Nursing homes	
Betting, Gaming and Lotteries Act 1963	Gambling and gaming	
Employment Agencies Act 1973	Employment agencies	
Children's Act 1975	Employment of children	
Town & Country Planning Acts 1963–84	Planning permission	

The local Borough or District Council handles planning permission, and a range of other licences such as:

Music and dancing

Late night refreshments
Cinema
Theatre employers
Theatre performance of plays
Pleasure boats
Lotteries and amusements
Amusements with prizes
Food and ice cream
Hawkers
Street and house-to-house collections
Petroleum and paint storage
Private hire vehicle operator
Private hire and hackney carriage driver's licence
Private hire and hackney carriage vehicle licence
Pet shop
Breeding of dogs
Boarding of dogs
Riding establishments
Slaughterman
Dealing in game
Scrap metal dealing
Explosives and fireworks
Shops and factories

Make first contact with the Planning Department or Environmental Health Department.

For public houses, licensed restaurants, hotels, boarding houses and wine bars, contact the Justices' Clerk.

Then there are optional – but often desirable – licences: ABTA for travel agents, and industry codes of practice, eg National Inspection Council for Electrical Installation Contracting, National Association of Funeral Directors.

Data protection

The Data Protection Act 1985 requires any business that keeps records of personal data on individuals in computer files to register with the government. Existing data files should be registered. New computerised records need immediate registration. Further information is available from the Office of the Data Protection Registrar, Springfield House, Water Lane, Wilmslow, Cheshire SK9 5AX; telephone 0625 535711.

Business insurance

In addition to the insurance that an individual will take out in his private life, there is a need for the businessman to consider seriously the insurance he will need at business start-up, and then throughout his business career. The following list is designed to help him decide which to take out, and when.

	Immediate cover (date)	To be covered by (date)	Not relevant in foreseeable future
1. Fire and special perils			
2. Advance and consequential loss following fire, special perils, sprinkler damage, and machinery breakdown			
3. Burglary			
4. Employer's liability			
5. Professional indemnity			
6. Directors' and Officers' liability			
7. Public and product liability			
8. Money			
9. Commercial vehicles			
10. Goods in transit			
11. Private cars			
12. Mobile plant			
13. Contractors all risks			
14. Engineering - lifting equipment, electrical plant boilers, and general equipment			
15. Plate glass			
16. Key man (including personal accident and sickness, private hospital costs), group personnel			
17. Life assurance and pensions			
18. Computer and computer records			
19. Legal costs and expenses			
20. Livestock			
21. Marine and aircraft insurance			
22. Political risk			
23. Credit insurance			
24. Fidelity			

Which of these covers are you *required by law* to take out?

Obtaining UK registered design protection

* In many cases products of an original design are protected from illicit copying by the Copyright, Designs and Patent Act. This protection is inherent and immediate.

Professional advice at an early stage will help you to assess the value and chances of obtaining design registration. Please see also the free official pamphlet 'Introducing Design Registration', available from the Patent Office, Information and Marketing Services, Cardiff Road, Newport, Gwent NP9 1RH.

Obtaining a UK patent

Because of the complex nature of the above, you should take professional advice.

Obtaining UK trade mark registration

A trade mark is a word, device etc, which is used to identify a trader's goods and to distinguish such goods from others. If the trade mark is sufficiently distinctive, statutory rights in it may be obtained through registration.

IS YOUR TRADE MARK FREE TO USE?

Conduct preliminary search of:

1. Marks in use on the same or similar goods

2. Marks already registered for those goods

3. Pending trade mark applications.

Obtain Registrar's advice on distinctiveness by filing Form TM29.

File application at Trade Marks Registry after deciding which Class is appropriate from the 34 Classes of goods. Forms TM2 and TM4.

Registry search of prior pending and registered similar marks.

Submit arguments to Registry objections and/or amendments.

Mark accepted/refused for registration.

If accepted, mark is advertised in the *Trade Marks Journal*, after which it may be opposed within *one month*. If unopposed, mark is registered for an initial period of 7 years, renewable for periods of 14 years thereafter.

Professional advice is strongly recommended in all matters relating to trade marks in view of the possibility of confusion and/or passing off occurring, with resultant litigation.

8

Beginning to Manage

Documentation for start-up

Paperwork should be kept to a minimum. Nevertheless, paper records are required to protect you and your business. Most of these items will be required before start-up:

	Dates		
	Designed	Ordered	Delivered
Letterhead			
Business card			
Publicity material			
Price-lists			
Order pad			
Invoice/delivery/credit note set			
Monthly statement			
Petty cash voucher book			
Cheque book			
Bank paying-in book			

The letterhead and business card may well be the first contact a customer has with your business.

Will they say about you what you want them to say?

In the case of a private limited company, the letterhead must show the address of the registered office, the registration number, and Limited or Ltd, all or none of the directors, VAT number if registered.

Basic business records

No business can be properly run without adequate records. This short list covers the *absolute minimum* of information. Records should be written up daily or weekly, and be completely backed up by receipts, vouchers etc.

1. *Cash book*
   (a) Record cash sales and payments made from cash transactions.
   (b) Record payments in and out of bank.
   (c) Show VAT on payments as applicable.

2. *VAT records* (if applicable)
   (a) Show how VAT return figures have been calculated.
   (b) In addition, non-retailers must maintain a list of sales invoices issued.

3. *Petty cash book* (where applicable)
   Small cash expenses should be kept on an imprest basis and should show VAT where applicable.

4. *Wages book, wage slips*
   Summary information to meet the needs of the employee and the Inland Revenue.

5. *Order and delivery books*
   Purchases and sales, orders and deliveries.

6. *Overdue accounts book*
   Debtors and age analysis of debts for all credit sales.

Professional advice *from your accountant* should establish the most appropriate records for the business. If you follow his advice, it will also tend to reduce his fees.

Some businesses may find the services provided by a contract book-keeping service cost-effective.

The bank account

Few businesses can operate outside the banking system. These details should be covered well before start-up date.

1. *How many accounts?*

	Needed (tick)	Date arranged	Note
Business current account			**Overdraft facility**
Business deposit account			**Interest rate?**
Business loan accounts			
Personal current account			
Personal deposit account			
Personal loan account			
Personal 'tax' account			**To cover future tax demands**

Don't have more accounts than you need and can manage.

2. *Bank statements*

   Frequency (delete as applicable)
   Daily
   Weekly
   Monthly, or
   Quarterly

   The bank reconciliation (see below) should be made for each statement.

3. *Signatories*
   Obtain bank mandate form.
   Use crossed cheques.
   Name two signatories whenever practicable.

   NB. Two signatories may lead the Inland Revenue to argue that a 'sole trader' is now a 'partnership'. Complete cheque book stubs fully and accurately.

4. *Charges*
   It all costs money. Discuss with your bank manager what you can sensibly do to minimise bank charges. Get quotations from other banks.

Bank reconciliations

A bank statement is produced by the bank at your request. A weekly statement would be right for many businesses.

A bank position or report shows your own latest figures of your bank account.

The *bank statement* and the *bank position or report* should be reconciled from time to time – often weekly. This format shows how to do the reconciliation.

1. Balance according to bank statement	£
2. Add monies paid in but not cleared by the bank (deduct if bank statement shows an overdraft)	£
3. Deduct cheques drawn but not entered by the bank (add if bank statement shows an overdraft)	£
4. Balance according to books	£
Difference, if any	£

Any difference should be investigated immediately.

NB. Interest on any overdraft, and bank charges, will be debited to the account automatically and usually every quarter.

Purchasing practice

Good purchasing is a vital element in all businesses but especially in retailing and manufacturing. This checklist has been designed as a guide to purchasing.

Action	Check
1. Analyse goods to be purchased	Specification complete, up to date and accurate
2. Identify vendors who can supply	Provision for quality assurance Competitiveness Financial status
3. Issue enquiries	Instructions clear Terms of purchase specified Delivery requirements Any additional requirements
4. Receipt of quotations	Equipment described meets specification Analyse vendor's 'Conditions of Sale' and compare with your 'Conditions of Purchase' Price variation or fixed price? Payment terms and quantity discounts/rebates Validity Warranty Delivery period
5. Evaluation of quotations	Comparisons 'like for like' Total cost of order in consideration of any advance payments Current workload/financial status Delivery period
6. Choose best option	After considering 4 and 5 above
7. Place order	Terms of order are agreeable to vendor and purchaser Any additional requirements
8. Expedite acknowledgement	Check 'Terms of Acknowledgement' are in agreement with 'Terms of Order'
9. Monitor progress of order	Inspection/expeditor reports as necessary
10. Approve invoice payment	Check goods received in good order Verify any extras/reductions Obtain Certificates of Ownership if appropriate.

The routine of business accounting

There is no substitute for keeping up to date financial control. Check that you meet these suggestions:

	Daily	Weekly	Monthly	Quarterly	Six-monthly
Check cash takings against till roll (Retail)	✓				
Note cash position	✓				
Write up day books	✓				
Raise invoices	✓				
Bank cash/cheques	✓				
Check deliveries against delivery notes	✓				
Pay wages		✓	or ✓		
Draw cheques		✓			
Prepare weekly summaries		✓			
Do bank reconciliation		✓	or ✓		
Follow up overdues		✓	✓		
Issue statements			✓		
Total and summarise ledgers			✓		
Authorise salaries, tax and NI			✓		
Compare actual with budgeted sales and expenses			✓		
Update cash flow projections			✓	or ✓	
Take raw material, work in progress and finished goods stocks			✓	or ✓	
Prepare age analysis of debtors and creditors		✓	or ✓		
Pay VAT				✓	
Prepare trading account			✓	or ✓	or ✓
Prepare interim accounts			✓	or ✓	or ✓
Complete tax planning				✓	or ✓
Do sales and expenses budget updates				✓	

Precisely who is responsible for each item of work?

How do you know it is being done properly and on time?

Annual accounts

Annual acounts should be completed within a few weeks of the financial year end, and include:

1. Profit and loss account
2. Balance sheet
3. Sources and application of funds (companies)
4. Notes and analyses
5. Directors' Reports (companies)

Annual accounts are a legal requirement for companies. Sole traders and partnerships need them for the taxman, and probably the bank. Usually they are prepared by your accountant.

Annual accounts provide insufficient information for the running of most businesses. To keep control of a business you must have constant up-to-date information, which should be discussed with your accountant.

	Tick your plan		
How often do you want to have:	**Monthly**	**Quarterly**	**Six-monthly**
Trading accounts	☐	☐	☐
Profit and loss accounts	☐	☐	☐
Balance sheets	☐	☐	☐
Sources and application of funds statements	☐	☐	☐
Working capital movements	☐	☐	☐
Summarised cash movements	☐	☐	☐
Cash flow projections	☐	☐	☐

Tick your plan

	Monthly	Quarterly	Six-monthly
Discussion of current trends and prospects	☐	☐	☐
Review of overall plans	☐	☐	☐

NB. Some of the above are alternatives depending on the amount of information considered necessary for effective control.

Marginal product costing

As a prelude to any sales, the businessman should calculate his cost build-up using a format similar to this.

Direct material costs

	Cost	×	Usage*	=	Materials cost
Materials	£ per unit	×	Units per product, job etc	=	£ per product, job etc
(i)					
(ii)					
(iii)					
(iv)					
(v)					
(vi)					
(vii)					
		Total Direct material cost (A)	=	£	

* Including wastage/losses

Direct labour costs

	Cost**	×	Usage		=	Labour cost
Operations	£ per unit	×	Standard hours per product, job etc		=	£ per product, job etc
(i)						
(ii)						
(iii)						
(iv)						
			Total Direct labour cost (B)		=	£

** Full cost, not wage rate

Total variable cost   C = (A) + (B) =   £ _____

Overhead costs

Annual Cost £

For example:
Marketing costs
Travel
Rent, rates
Insurance
Post, telephone
Heating, lighting
Repairs, maintenance
Administration salaries, NI
Professional fees
Loan and overdraft interest
Depreciation
Others

Total cost	_____	(D)

Products

	1	2	3 etc		
Selling price (£)					(E)
Product, jobs etc (number)					(F)
Total sales (£)					(G = E × F)
Total direct materials (£)					(H = A × F)
Total direct labour (£)					(I = B × F)
Total variable cost (£)					(J = H + I)

Contribution to overheads
and profit (£)   (K = G - J)

═══   ═══   ═══

Overhead cost
(£)   (D)

─────────

Profit (£)   (K - D)

═════════

Gross margin =
%

$\dfrac{\text{Contribution} \times 100}{\text{£ Sales}}$ $(\dfrac{K}{G} \times 100)$

────   ────   ────   ─────────

These figures may help with:

- New price structures
- Changes to product mix
- Adjustments to size of labour force
- Make or buy-in decisions
- Capital expenditure to save labour costs

Margins and mark-ups

Business people involved with retailers need to be familiar with these two
expressions.

Margin = $\dfrac{\text{Selling price - buying price}}{\text{Selling price}} \times 100 =$ %

Mark-up = $\dfrac{\text{Selling price - buying price}}{\text{Buying price}} \times 100 =$ %

Try these calculations:

Selling price (excl VAT)	Buying price (excl VAT)	Percentage margin	Percentage mark-up
£1.00	50p		
£1.50	£1.00		
£2.66	£2.00		
£3.00	£2.40		
£4.00	£3.60		

Cash collection

A sale is not a sale until it is paid for (although it will go into your accounts as soon as it is invoiced)!

Wherever credit is given, cash flow can *always* be improved – by improved cash collection.

Improve cash collection by

1. Having a named person responsible for cash collection.

2. Setting cash collection targets and measuring performance.

3. Taking out credit references and setting credit limits.

4. Specifying payment date on:

   - quotation/estimate
   - price-list
   - delivery note (file signed copy)
   - invoice statement

   And mentioning it in all relevant conversations.

5. Issuing invoice immediately and accurately on completion/delivery of work. Cross reference to order numbers. Deliver to correct address as specified by the buyer.

6. Establishing date of automatic follow-up by:

   - statement
   - letter of demand
   - telephone   Don't be taken in by excuses!
   - stop supply
   - letter of legal action

7. Considering prompt payment discounts, deposits, prepayments and stage payments.

8. Proceedings through:

   County Court (Limit £5,000)
      Small claims procedure (Limit £500)
   High Court.

9. Pressing for execution of any court order.

10. Ceasing to supply slow payers on credit: use proforma invoice.

11. Considering non-recourse factoring and bad debt insurance.

Is credit given measured?

Days

1. $\dfrac{\text{Total outstandings} \times 365}{\text{Annual sales}} =$

   or

2. Total outstandings offset against immediate past invoives =

3. What were comparable figures:

   last year?

   in previous year?

4. What do competitors give?

The integrated computer accounting package

To the question 'Should I buy an integrated computer accounting system?' there is no immediate answer.

Take expert advice, and remember that *rarely will the computer bring cost reductions,* but it may enable more work to be handled.

Interrelations in the integrated package

In a fully integrated computer accounting package, the full range of accounting functions – sales, purchases, accounting, P&L accounts, trial balances, stock control and the rest – can be handled. In this diagram, the way in which these functions interrelate is shown.

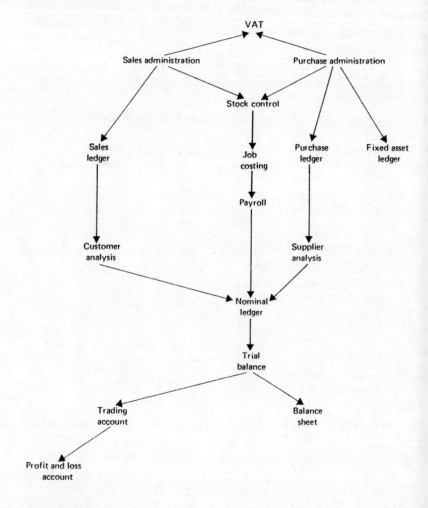

Credit cards

From the point of view of a merchant or trader, the use of a credit card can be a considerable advantage. Following on the well-known Visa and Access cards, progressive towns such as Wilmslow in Cheshire have now introduced their own charge card.

Advantages of the credit card

1. The merchant obtains immediate credit on depositing the sales voucher with the appropriate bank or finance house.

2. The funds are normally credited without recourse, thereby eliminating a guarantee of payment by telephone.

3. As an easy and trouble-free method of payment, it can attract a custom which might not otherwise have been forthcoming.

4. Mail and telephone order facilities may be available to the merchant. Retailers' own cards are also available.

5. The bulk of the administration is done centrally, and there is little or no necessity for extra resources to maintain accounts.

6. Normally only one VAT invoice is required each month for the commission.

7. Sales vouchers of £10 and under are normally accepted as VAT invoices, and this ensures that paperwork in relation to VAT is then kept to an absolute minimum.

8. Company credit cards are now available for directors and employees to meet their expenses for payment by direct debit. This scheme features personalised cards for the authorised company employee, produces a company statement, and narrative memoranda for each company employee. These are sent to the company monthly and give the company an average of 17 days' credit.

9. Both the supplier and the lender are liable to credit card users buying goods and/or services for £100 or more.

Costs of the credit card

1. There is normally a joining fee, paid only once. For example, the VAT inclusive charge for a credit card varies from £20 to £100.

2. There is a service charge on each transaction, which falls on the trader; it is normally between 3 and 5 per cent.

3. Be sure that the cost of accepting credit card transactions does not unacceptably reduce your mark-up (for example, on a single low-cost item with an already slender margin).

4. For company credit cards there are various conditions, including an overall credit limit. Costs range from either £3 per annum per card, and 20p per debit entry, to £12 per annum per card, with no entry charge.

Obtaining a credit card facility

1. Application to the issuing bank or finance house.

2. Visit by credit card consultant.

3. Completion of essential details on application form.

4. Acceptance.

Which of these British Telecom services will you use?

Note that calls to 0800 numbers are free.

Facility	Apply	Service
Bureaufax	Area Sales Office or dial 100 and ask for Freefone BTI	Facsimile service in the UK and abroad. To send or receive facsimile copies of documents
Confravision	Area Sales Office	Conference service between distant points by television
Freefone	Dial 0800 345800	Client can now sell their service, products or company image. No numbers to be remembered by a customer. Freefone name encourages people to get in touch
International packet switching service Timenet Packet switch stream	Global Network Services, dial 0800 181 555 or 0800 282 444	Data communications service. Wide variety of communication needs and applications. Linked to numerous international computer networks Public data service. Widely used for computer communication
Prestel	Sales dial 0800 200 700 Help-line dial 0442 237 237	Public viewdata service. Includes information mailbox. Links adapted television screens to computers through ordinary telephone lines
Telecom Gold	Dial 0800 282 4444	24-hour public electronic mail service
Telex equipment	Dial 0800 444 145	Hard copy print out of communications keyboarded by sender
External lines Business Residential	Area Sales Office	Products & Services: for the business for the home

A range of telephone services is also available from Mercury: New Mercury House, 26 Red Lion Square, London WC1R 4HQ; 071-528 2028.

Mail services

Can your business survive with the Royal Mail? In addition to the basic delivery service, the Post Office provides a range of additional services. Which of the following will help your business? Current prices are available in the 'Postal Rates' booklet. Local Business Centres are given in phone books, local directories or located via directory enquiries.

Facility	Apply	Service	Notes
PO Box number	Local Business Centre	Collect or deliver letters and parcels	Provides earlier availability of correspondence
Business reply	Form P2797	1st or 2nd class mail	Application needs sample envelope
Freepost	Form P2797	1st or 2nd class mail	Usually for direct response sales campaigns
Recorded delivery	Post Office Counter	Signed delivery	Provides proof of delivery
Registered post	Post Office Counter	Insured, signed delivery	Mainly for valuables. First class mail only
Franking machines	Six manufacturers	Mail out franking	Rental or purchase agreed with manufacturer. Gives advertising and security benefits
Datapost	0800 224 466	Same day collection and delivery between most UK business centres	Cash or credit. Also international up to 30 kg per item. Not for high value goods
Special delivery	Post Office Counter	Next day delivery	Excludes Channel Islands, Isle of Man, where Express Delivery Service applies
COD	Post Office Counter	Cash on delivery	Must be registered (letters or parcels)
Household delivery	National enquiry centre 0865 780400	Leaflet delivery to every letter box in area; targets may be specified as business or residential	
Parcels	Post Office Counter	Three day service	Also local routes, max 30 kg. Size limits apply

Facility	Apply	Service	Notes
Direct mail Mail Sort	Local Business Centre	Same day posting	
Bulk rebate service	Postal Sales Representative	Delivery within seven days excluding weekends	Rebates on pre-sorted mailings over 4000 letters at one time, on a sliding scale from 15 to 30 per cent

9

Employment

Sources of employees

As an aid to finding the appropriately qualified person for employment, this list has been prepared:

- Existing employees
- Other businesses
- Relatives and friends
- Jobcentre
- Careers Office
- Placement Officers at schools, colleges and polytechnics
- Youth Training: Managing agents, Jobcentre, or Careers Office
- Job advertisements – local press, radio/TV
- Recruitment and placement agencies
- Personnel managers handling a redundancy programme

Planning the employment interview

In view of the high costs to the business of poor recruitment, this list is a summary of the minimum essential preparation.

Is there a *written*: Job Description?

Personal Profile?

What *must* you learn from the interview?

....

....

List the following:

Rates of pay - immediate - after training - overtime - bonuses, commissions
Hours of work/working week - breaks
Holidays
Other benefits - vehicle - health insurance - pension

Have you checked:

- How income tax will be deducted? ☐
- National Insurance? ☐
- Statutory Sick Pay? ☐
- Statutory Maternity Pay? ☐
- Equal Opportunities and similar legislation? ☐

Can the workplace be visited?

Who will make up the interviewing team?

....

....

....

Personal profile

The employment of the right person in a small business is vital. The table opposite may be used to assess prospective employees, partners, working directors, and even, to an extent, new shareholders.

This profile will help a business to remain within Equal Opportunities and Sex Discrimination legislation.

Does your application form help you to get this information?

Qualifications for employment	
Required (= must have)	Desirable (= nice to have)

1. Age
2. Education
3. Training
4. Experience
5. Abilities/skills
6. Ambitions/future
7. Attitudes
8. Marital status
9. Health
10. Location

Employees' statutory rights

For employees working more than 16 hours per week and for those working between 8 and 16 hours per week, and subject to various lengths of service, there are statutory rights in respect of:

1. Written particulars of the terms of employment

2. Wage or salary pay statement

3. Notice of termination of employment

4. Time off for public duties

5. Provisions in connection with pregnancy, maternity and the right to return to work

6. Guaranteed payments

7. Payment when suspended on medical grounds

8. Redundancy

9. Dismissal

10. Statutory Maternity Pay (SMP)

11. Statutory Sick Pay (SSP)

12. The health and safety at work and anti-discrimination legislation apply to all employees, regardless of their hours of work and length of service.

Taking on an employee

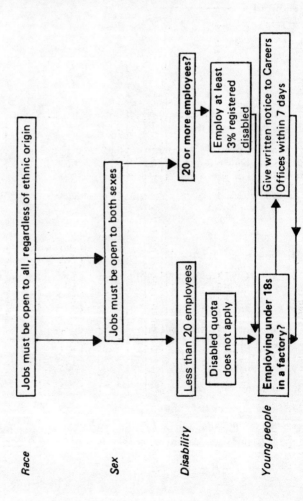

Notes

Race

Exemptions. Genuine occupational qualifications, private households, training in skills to be used abroad, seamen recruited abroad, Northern Ireland. Some are likely to be removed, so check.

Sex

Exemptions. Only if worker's sex can be shown to be a genuine occupational qualification, eg acting role, private households, communal accommodation.

Young people

Consult Jobcentre if unable to do so

Race — Jobs must be open to all, regardless of ethnic origin

Sex — Jobs must be open to both sexes

20 or more employees? → Employ at least 3% registered disabled

Disability — Less than 20 employees → Disabled quota does not apply

Young people — Employing under 18s in a factory? → Give written notice to Careers Offices within 7 days

Written statement of main terms and conditions of employment

Employee works at least 16 hours per week?

Must provide written statement of main terms and conditions of employment within 13 weeks of employment

To include main terms and conditions, pay, holidays, details of notice and discipline procedures (seek help from ACAS).

Employee works 8-16 hours per week?

Must provide written statement after 5 years

No obligation to provide statement

Men and women must get same pay for equivalent work

Wages

Does Agricultural Wages Board apply?

Minimum rates payable

Wage rates uncontrolled, but have regard to any collective agreement

Ask at Jobcentre or of Agricultural Wages Board (3–8 Whitehall Place, London SW1A 2HH; 071-270 8535). Wages Councils are due to be phased out; in the meantime rates are obtainable from the Secretary of the appropriate Council (Steel House, 11 Tothill Street, London SW1H 9NF. 071-273 4812).

135

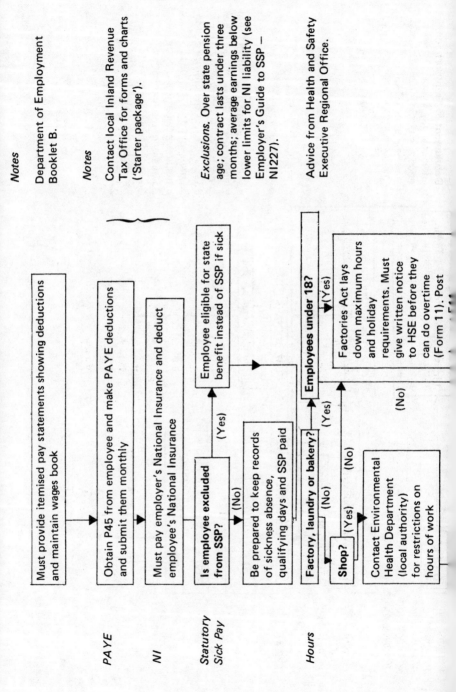

Notes

Department of Employment Booklet B.

Notes

Contact local Inland Revenue Tax Office for forms and charts ('Starter package').

Exclusions. Over state pension age; contract lasts under three months; average earnings below lower limits for NI liability (see Employer's Guide to SSP – NI227).

Advice from Health and Safety Executive Regional Office.

PAYE

Must provide itemised pay statements showing deductions and maintain wages book

Obtain P45 from employee and make PAYE deductions and submit them monthly

NI

Must pay employer's National Insurance and deduct employee's National Insurance

Statutory Sick Pay

Is employee excluded from SSP?

(Yes) → Employee eligible for state benefit instead of SSP if sick

(No) → Be prepared to keep records of sickness absence, qualifying days and SSP paid

Hours

Factory, laundry or bakery?

(Yes) → Employees under 18?

(Yes) → Factories Act lays down maximum hours and holiday requirements. Must give written notice to HSE before they can do overtime (Form 11). Post...

(No) → Shop?

(Yes) → Contact Environmental Health Department (local authority) for restrictions on hours of work

(No)

136

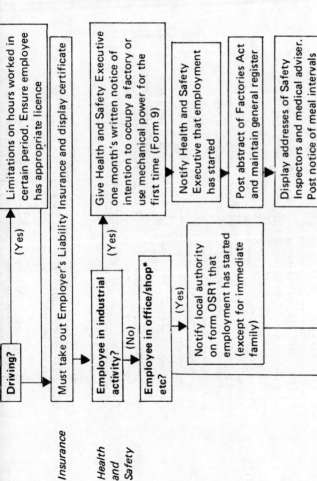

Department of Transport booklet.

Insurance broker or insurance company.

* Includes wholesalers, warehouses, public catering and fuel storage

Contact Health and Safety Executive Regional office for details of other notices to be posted in particular industries.

Driving?

(Yes) → Limitations on hours worked in certain period. Ensure employee has appropriate licence

Insurance

Must take out Employer's Liability Insurance and display certificate

Health and Safety

Employee in industrial activity?

(Yes) → Give Health and Safety Executive one month's written notice of intention to occupy a factory or use mechanical power for the first time (Form 9)

(No) ↓

Employee in office/shop* etc?

(Yes) → Notify local authority on form OSR1 that employment has started (except for immediate family)

→ Notify Health and Safety Executive that employment has started

→ Post abstract of Factories Act and maintain general register

→ Display addresses of Safety Inspectors and medical adviser. Post notice of meal intervals and clock used

→ **50 or more employees?**

Post notice OSR9

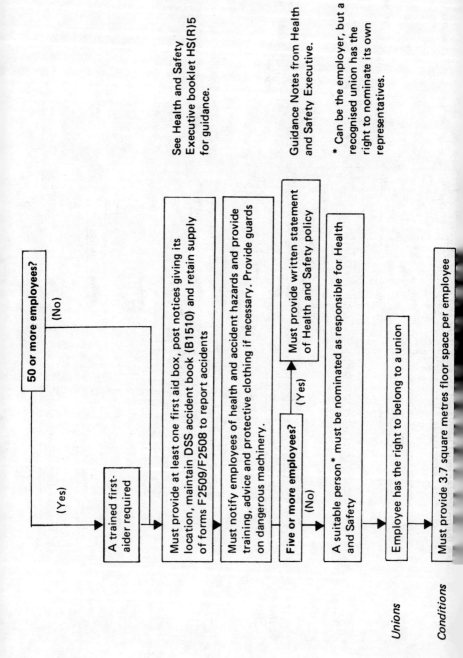

50 or more employees?

(Yes) (No)

A trained first-aider required

Must provide at least one first aid box, post notices giving its location, maintain DSS accident book (B1510) and retain supply of forms F2509/F2508 to report accidents

Must notify employees of health and accident hazards and provide training, advice and protective clothing if necessary. Provide guards on dangerous machinery.

See Health and Safety Executive booklet HS(R)5 for guidance.

Five or more employees?

(No) (Yes)

Must provide written statement of Health and Safety policy

A suitable person* must be nominated as responsible for Health and Safety

Guidance Notes from Health and Safety Executive.

* Can be the employer, but a recognised union has the right to nominate its own representatives.

Unions

Employee has the right to belong to a union

Conditions

Must provide 3.7 square metres floor space per employee

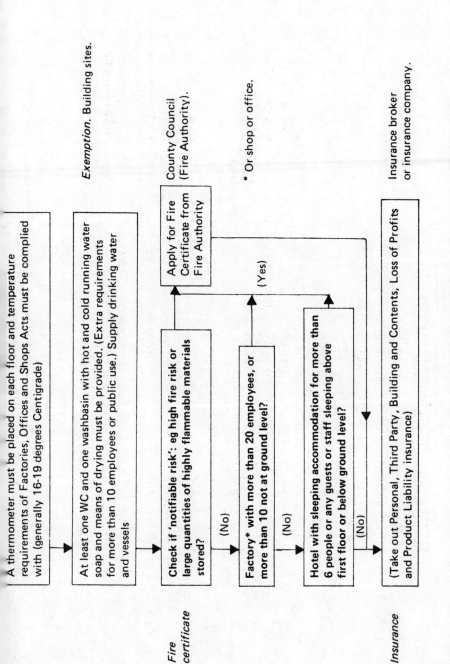

A thermometer must be placed on each floor and temperature requirements of Factories, Offices and Shops Acts must be complied with (generally 16-19 degrees Centigrade)

At least one WC and one washbasin with hot and cold running water soap and means of drying must be provided. (Extra requirements for more than 10 employees or public use.) Supply drinking water and vessels

Fire certificate

Check if 'notifiable risk': eg high fire risk or large quantities of highly flammable materials stored?

(No)

Factory* with more than 20 employees, or more than 10 not at ground level?

(No)

(Yes)

Hotel with sleeping accommodation for more than 6 people or any guests or staff sleeping above first floor or below ground level?

(No)

Apply for Fire Certificate from Fire Authority

Exemption. Building sites.

County Council (Fire Authority).

* Or shop or office.

Insurance

(Take out Personal, Third Party, Building and Contents, Loss of Profits and Product Liability insurance)

Insurance broker or insurance company.

139

Pay As You Earn (PAYE) and National Insurance (NI)

Immediately, in the case of a limited company, and very early in the life of a sole trader, the business must act as a tax gatherer for the government. This flow chart shows the weekly, monthly and annual routines to be observed.

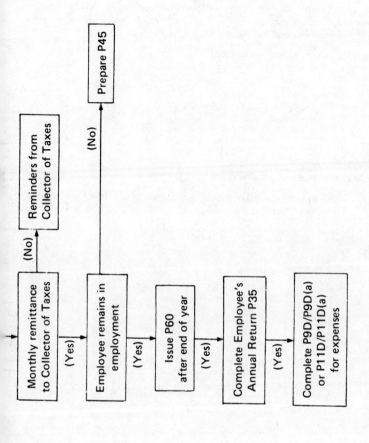

Further help may be drawn from the Tax Office, DSS, your accountant or commercial payroll services.

The business should have a legal adviser capable of providing guidance to ensure proper respect for employment law. The solicitor would also act for the business when an employee or former employee made claims arising from termination of employment or disciplinary action.

NB. Businesses employing *fewer than 20 persons* have no requirement to employ disabled persons.

Additional reference
Employment Protection (Consolidation) Act 1978.

National Insurance payments

All four classes of National Insurance contributions could affect the smaller business. These flowcharts show how payments should be handled.

Class 1 contributions for employed persons

NB. Directors are also employees. Reduced contributions are payable by those who hold a Certificate of Election or a Certificate of Reduced Liability.

Class 2 contributions for self-employed persons

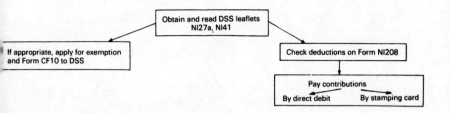

NB. Self-employed persons are *not* eligible for Unemployed Benefit, Industrial Injuries Benefit or earnings related benefits.

Class 3 contributions

Class 3 contributions are voluntary, and may be made by persons not gainfully employed in Great Britain. The fixed contribution may be paid by:

- Direct debit
- Stamping a card
- Lump sum payment at end of tax year.

Class 4 contributions for self-employed persons

Class 4 contributions are akin to an additional income tax. The contributions are collected by the Inland Revenue alongside Schedule D liabilities and relate to taxable profits between upper and lower limits.

Statutory Sick Pay (SSP)

The SSP Scheme has been in force since 6 April 1983. For those not familiar with its operation, their solicitor or accountant will provide help. These notes provide a brief introduction to the subject. Please see also leaflet NI 227.

Employee	Employer	*Notes*
	Establish notification rules and qualifying dates	
Goes sick		
Phones to –	Nominated person	Appointed to note absence
	Logs in	
	Absence record	Official record of absence, can be inspected by DSS. Contains other basic details of QUALIFYING DAYS PAYMENTS – to be kept for three years

Returns to work Completes ABSENCE STATEMENT Provides DOCTOR'S NOTE for absences above 7 days	Retains document(s)	
	Makes SSP payments	Record on Form P11
	Deducts SSP payments made from settlement with Inland Revenue	
	Annual summary	Use Form P14

Statutory Maternity Pay (SMP)

These notes provide a brief guide and your solicitor and accountant will help. Please see also leaflet NI 257.

Employee	Employer	*Notes*
	Establish notification rules and qualifying dates	
21 days before expected week of confinement (EWC) or as soon as practicable, informs and gives evidence of pregnancy in FORM MATB1 or doctor's certificate	Nominated Person logs in Absence Record	Appointed to note absence
Chooses when pay to start	Make SMP payments for 12 weeks starting any week from 11th to 6th week before EWC	
Must give 21 days' written notice of intention to return to work	Retains documents	Official record of payments can be inspected by DSS
	Deducts SMP payments from settlement with Inland Revenue	
	Can require confirmation of return at least 49 days before EWC	

Subcontractors' tax certificates

For some industries, notably the construction industry, there are benefits to both the contractor and the subcontractor if the latter holds a 714 certificate (Department of Employment).

1. *Start-up as an uncertified subcontractor.*

   Contractor deducts tax at 25 per cent, Form SC60.
   Contractor pays deductions to Inland Revenue.
   Subcontractor registers as self-employed with local tax office.
   Inland Revenue makes adjustments after end of tax year.
   Subcontractor pays own Class 2 National Insurance contribution.
   Subcontractor signs off DSS benefits.

2. *Subcontractor applies for 714 certificate:* the authorities are unlikely to issue a 714 until some significant time after the start-up.

   Subcontractor must be UK based in relevant industry.
   Subcontractor must have good record of employment.
   Subcontractor must have good record of tax and NI contribution payments.
   Subcontractor must have proper business records and facilities.

3. *Certified subcontractor advises contractor.*

   Relieves contractor of administration.
   Subcontractor issues 715 voucher for every payment.
   Subcontractor maintains necessary records.
   Subcontractor makes returns to Inspector of Taxes.

NB. The 714 Certificate exists in four forms:

For individuals	714I
For partnerships	714P
For certain companies	714C
For special situations	714S

The *contractor* has an obligation to check:

- Names and photographs on 714I, 714P, 714S
- Expiry date
- Identity of bearer

to avoid tax liability.

Health and safety at work: Checklist

Under the Health and Safety at Work Act 1974, the employer (even if he is self-employed) has major responsibilities which may be tested through these questions. Both your solicitor and the Health and Safety Executive can help with uncertainties.

The location

Access	Is it adequate?
Neighbours	Will they harm your staff (dust, smell, noise etc)?
	Will you harm their staff (dust, smell, noise etc)?

The premises

Space	Is it big enough?
Ventilation	Is it adequate?
Heating	Is it adequate?
Lighting	Is it adequate?

Electrical installation	Is it in good condition?
Fire precautions	Are escapes marked and assembly areas identified?
	Are fire extinguishers of correct type?
	Is a fire alarm fitted and tested?
Floors, stairs	Are they sound and non-slip?
Toilets	Are they in a satisfactory condition?
	Are there enough?
Safety audit	When was it last done?

Equipment

First aid	Have you got a first aid kit? Safety showers? Protective gear?
Machinery	Is it properly installed?
	Is it properly guarded?
Statutory inspections	Has a surveyor from your insurers examined your:
	– air receiver or compressor
	– steam boiler
	– lifting tackle
	– cranes
	– lifts
	– pressure vessels?

Materials handled

Toxic	Are precautions adequate?
	Effluents and waste disposal?
Inflammable*	Are precautions adequate?
	Flameproof equipment?
Corrosive	Are precautions adequate?
Dust/fume control	Is local exhaust ventilation required?
Protective clothing	Is any required? Is it issued and used?

* Flammable has the same meaning, ie easily set on fire.

Environment

Noise	Is your process very noisy?
	What precautions do you need to take?

Systems of work

Methods of work	Are they carefully thought out?
	Are they safe?
Training	Do your employees know what to do?
	Have they been warned about potential risks and the precautions to be taken?
	What is the existing pattern of evacuation drills?
Supervision	How do you make sure they work in accordance with instructions?

Others

Safety	If you have more than five employees, then you must have a written safety policy.
Safety representatives	If you have a recognised trade union, they may appoint safety representatives.
Notification of accidents	If a serious accident happens in your premises, you must inform the relevant authority as soon as possible.

Forms

If your premises are subject to the Factories Act 1961 or Offices, Shops and Railway Premises Act 1963, then you must display an abstract of the relevant Act at your premises. If you intend to open a factory you must notify the Health and Safety Executive of your intention not less than 28 days before you open it.

10

Are Big Problems on the Way?

Overtrading, a problem associated with success

Some problems arise from *success*. Difficulties may be caused by expanding the business more quickly than cash resources can stand. This is *overtrading*.

This checklist may help you decide whether overtrading is a threat to your business.

Tick those which apply to your business

Customers clamouring for goods ☐

Stocks increasing ☐

Debtors increasing ☐

Creditors crying out for payment ☐

Suppliers threatening to cut off supplies ☐

Overdraft limit breached: bank refusing to lend more ☐

For remedies, see opposite page.

The cash flow problem

Possible causes

| Rapid sales expansion (overtrading) | Raw material cost inflation | Major bad debts | Sales decline | Expenses growth | Heavy capital expenditure |

The cash flow problem is a symptom not a cause. This chart may help to avoid it. Try to start from position X — too many start from position Y.

X → Regular cash flow projections

Y → Delayed recognition of problem — no cash flow projection available

Breach overdraft facility limit → Letters from bank manager → Bank dishonours cheques

Identify cause

Delayed payments to creditors

See bank manager

Delayed payments to Inland Revenue, VAT

Bank reduces overdraft

External cash sources
1. Increased overdraft
2. Restructured finance
3. New equity

Internal cash generation
1. Reduce debtors
2. Negotiate increased creditors
3. Minimise capital expenditure
4. Sale of unproductive assets
5. Reduction of direct costs
6. Overhead reduction
7. Better stock management
8. Stock liquidation
9. Sale and leaseback
10. Improved production management
11. Concentrate on most profitable lines
12. Increase prices
13. Factoring of book debts

Default on loan repayments

Cannot pay the wages

Crash programme of cash improvement

Creditors' meeting

Bank calls in overdraft

Regular cash flow projections

Receivership or liquidation

Take to the bank proof of what you have already done to improve the situation

149

Growth, survival or extinction?

Knowing where the business is has consistently proved to be a key to survival in difficult markets and growth in buoyant ones. Pages 151–61 give simple formats for control information in typical smaller businesses. The items are set out in this order:

Responsibilities of the management
Sales and marketing effectiveness
Orders and shipments
Employment status
Cash

  Liquidity
  Debtors
  Creditors

Profitability

  Profit and loss account
  Break-even

Assets

  Balance sheet
  Control ratios

Business planning

  Cash flow projections
  Financial planning
  Management action plan

ARE BIG PROBLEMS ON THE WAY?

Responsibilities of the management

Who is responsible for:	To whom responsible?	Date of last report
Cash management		
Cash collection		
Costing		
Management information		
Accounts and book-keeping		
Invoicing		
Sales		
Marketing		
Pricing		
Customer complaints		
Employee relations		
Recruitment		
Security		
Production		
– costs		
– quality		
– rate		
Purchasing		
Other key elements in the business		

Sales and marketing effectiveness

	Last month		Prior month		Year to date	
	Number	Value of (monthly) business	Number	Value of (monthly) business	Number	Value of (monthly) business
New accounts won						
Existing accounts lost						
Enquiries obtained						
Quotations put out						
Firm orders gained						
Firm orders as repeat business						
Tenders notified						
Tenders submitted						
Tenders awarded						
Market trends reported in national regional local statistics						

Orders and shipments

Firm and despatchable orders on hand:

Volume _____ units

Value £

	Orders completed			Orders booked for completion			
						Forward months	
	3 months ago	2 months ago	Last month	This month	2	3	4
High contribution products £							
Medium contribution products £							
Low contribution products £							
Total sales £							
Gross margin £							
Overheads £							
Gross Margin – Overheads £							
Factory or business loading %							
Orders not despatched							
– supplier fault £							
– our fault £							

Employment status

	Last month	Prior month	Year to date
Desired number of employees			
Full time		—	
Part time	—	—	
TOTAL Full-time equivalents			
Employed at month end			
Vacancies unfilled			
Employees departed in month			
Resigned			
Dismissed			
Redundant			
Retired			
New employees recruited			
Absenteeism rate			

Cash

LIQUIDITY

	Now	Last week	Prior week	Last month
Cash in hand				
Balance per bank statement				
Payments drawn, not presented to bank				
Collections not credited to bank account				
Adjusted bank position				
Overdraft limit agreed with bank				

DEBTORS

	Last month	Prior month	Previous month
Total debtors (a)			
Moving annual sales + VAT (b)			
$\dfrac{\text{Debtors}}{\text{Sales}} = \dfrac{(a)}{(b)} \times 100$	%	%	%

In seasonal businesses, these percentages should be compared with figures from the corresponding period in past years.

CREDITORS

	Last month	Prior month	Previous month
Trade creditors (c)			
Moving annual trade purchases (d)			
$\dfrac{\text{Creditors}}{\text{Purchases}} = \dfrac{(c)}{(d)} \times 100$	%	%	%

In seasonal businesses, these percentages should be compared with figures from the corresponding period in past years.

Profitability

PROFIT AND LOSS ACCOUNT

	Current month				Financial Year to date			
	Last year	This year				Last year	This year	
	Actual	Actual	Budget			Actual	Actual	Budget	Variance
Sales								
Cost of sales								
Gross margin (B)								
Selling costs								
Distribution costs								
Administration costs								
Occupational costs								
Research and development costs								
Total overhead costs (A)								
Profit before interest and tax								
Interest								
Profit before tax								

BREAK-EVEN

Total overheads (A)
Gross margin % (B)
Break-even sales:
$\frac{A}{B} \times 100$

Assets

BALANCE SHEET

	Last financial year end	Last interim report	Current interim report
Fixed assets			
Land, buildings			
Fixtures, fittings and equipment			
Motor vehicles			
Total fixed assets			
Investments			
Current assets			
Stock			
Prepayments			
Debtors			
Bank			
Cash			
Total current assets			
Total assets			
Current liabilities			
Creditors – Trade			
– Others			
Accruals			
Overdraft			
Total current liabilities			
Long-term liabilities			
Proprietor's capital (net worth)			
Total liabilities and net worth			

CONTROL RATIOS

MAT is used below to stand for Moving Annual Total, ie, running 12-month figures.

	Last financial year end	Last interim report	Current interim report

Liquidity

$$\frac{\text{Current assets}}{\text{Current liabilities}}$$

$$\frac{\text{Current assets} - \text{Stock}}{\text{Current liabilities}}$$

Working capital

$$\frac{\text{Stock}}{\text{MAT cost of sales}}$$

$$\frac{\text{Debtors}}{\text{MAT sales}} \times 100\% \text{ (see page 157)}$$

$$\frac{\text{Creditors}}{\text{MAT purchases}} \times 100\% \text{ (see page 158)}$$

Financial structure

$$\frac{\text{Total liabilities}}{\text{Net worth}}$$

$$\frac{\text{MAT profit before interest and tax}}{\text{MAT interest paid}}$$

Profitability

$$\frac{\text{MAT profit before interest and tax}}{\text{Total assets}}$$

$$\frac{\text{MAT profit before interest and tax}}{\text{MAT sales}}$$

$$\frac{\text{MAT sales}}{\text{Total assets}}$$

Business planning
CASH FLOW PROJECTIONS

	This month	Month 2	3	4	5	6	etc
Opening balance (reconciled)							
Cash receipts							
Total inflow							
Cash payments							
Total outflow							
Closing balance							
Agreed bank overdraft facility							

FINANCIAL PLANNING

At the heart of business planning is forecast performance in these three areas:

	Current year by month	Next year by quarter	Following year
Cash flow (for format for first six months see above)	✓	✓	✓
Profit and loss account	✓	✓	✓
Balance sheet	✓	✓	✓

MANAGEMENT ACTION PLAN

Arising from the foregoing analyses, an action plan can be drawn up and assigned.

Major objectives*	To be done by	Completion date

* Clear and understandable
  Challenging but attainable
  Measurable
  Relevant
  Consistent with other objectives.

161

Heading for business ruin

Business failure runs at 80 per cent of all start-ups within their first five years. Studies like John Argenti's (in *Corporate Collapse – the Causes and the Symptoms*, McGraw-Hill, 1976) have shown identifying marks. *Score your enterprise* by marking NIL where you are uncertain whether the item is clearly visible in your business. Where the item is clearly visible, score the points indicated. There are no *in between* scores.

Defects *If they are clearly visible in your enterprise, score the marks in the next column*		*Your score*
Management		
1. Autocratic boss who dominates his colleagues and takes no advice from them.	8	
2. The boss is also the chairman.	4	
3. Passive board of management not actively participating in decisions.	2	
4. Skills on the board are unbalanced, eg there are too many engineers	2	
5. No competent, strong-minded finance man guiding the business.	2	
6. Where relevant, no depth of management below the board.	1	
Accounting		
1. No budget (If there is, it is not compared with actual each month.)	3	
2. No cash flow plan (If there is, it is out of date.)	3	
3. No costing system: no one knows what each product really costs, nor its cash contribution to overheads.	3	
Response to change		
The enterprise exhibits some clear and vital example of failing to respond to change, eg: – An ageing product – Old-fashioned plant – Out-of-date marketing – Outmoded attitude to employees – Ageing management – No computer	15	
TOTAL FOR DEFECTS	43	

Mistakes *If they are clearly visible in your enterprise, score the marks in the next column*		*Your score*
Leverage The *capital gearing* (external borrowing: proprietor's funds), *or* The *income gearing* (profit before interest and tax: interest) of the enterprise is noticeably high.	15	
Overtrading Turnover is rising at a much faster rate than the finance available to fund it.	15	
Projects The enterprise has launched a project (eg building a factory, launching a new major product, guaranteeing a subsidiary company's loan) of such a size that if it goes wrong it will bring down the enterprise.	15	
TOTAL FOR MISTAKES	45	

Symptoms of failure *If they are clearly visible in your enterprise, score these marks*		*Your score*
Financial signs Control ratios are deteriorating and cash is becoming extremely scarce.	4	
Creative accounting Accounts show evidence of window dressing to 'improve' profits, eg stocks valued higher, depreciation lower, repairs capitalised etc.	4	
Non-financial signs of distress Examples: Office needs painting, top management salaries frozen, capital expenditure decisions delayed, product quality or service deteriorating, morale failing.	3	
Nose-dive Impossible to hide the last-gasp scramble for survival: writs, rumours, resignations.	1	
TOTAL FOR SYMPTOMS OF FAILURE	12	
GRAND TOTAL	100	

Is your score 25 or above?

If so, there are grounds for serious concern about the future of your business. *Now* is the time to get additional help from your accountant, bank manager, the Small Firms Service, or your Local Enterprise Agency.

Profit improvement

The break-even chart on page 79 helps us to understand the *five* basic ways
of improving profitability:

Key
Dotted line = projected figures
Unbroken line = current figures

1. *Increase selling prices*

Increase prices with nil or acceptable decrease in sales volume to reduce the
break-even volume – but see page 79.

2. *Reduce variable costs*

Reduce direct materials and/or direct labour costs to reduce variable costs.
Thus total costs fall and reduce the break-even volume – see page 122.

3. *Reduce overheads (fixed costs)*

Reduce overheads to reduce total costs, in turn reducing the break-even
volume – see page 122.

4. *Increase sales volume*

Move up the sales line by selling more without disturbing selling prices, fixed or variable costs. All sales above break-even volume yield a profit. Therefore, the higher the volume, the higher the profit if all the other items remain constant – see pages 58–63.

5. *Improve product mix*

Concentrate on more profitable lines – often selling less in total – but also making correspondingly greater reductions in variable costs to reduce the break-even volume (see pages 48–9 and 79).

These are the only ways of increasing profitability

The end

The biggest losses are incurred by *'pouring good money after bad'*.

Sometimes the financial problem is one of cash where creditors cannot be paid, though asset values exceed all liabilities. Where the business is simply not paying its way early action is important to avoid debts running higher than necessary. Creditors will often wait for asset sales if they are kept informed of plans and progress by the proprietor. Full communication with creditors is essential.

At the *very* end, there are just a small number of *options*:

Limited company

Procedure	Instigated by	Requirements	Method
1. Voluntary Composition in satisfaction of debts or scheme of arrangement of affairs	Directors (unless company being wound up or subject to an administration order), approved by members and creditors	Solvency or insolvency, ie liabilities *Including* contingent and prospective liabilities exceed assets	Directors nominate supervisor who reports to court
2. Administration order	Members' and/or directors' and/or creditors' application for Court order	Potential or actual insolvency	Court appoints administrator
3. Administrative receivership	Creditor secured by floating charge	Breach of loan agreement	Administrative receiver appointed under terms of loan agreement
4. Receivership	Creditor secured by fixed charge	Breach of loan agreement	Receiver appointed under terms of loan agreement *or* by the court
5. Application to Court for winding up Court order	Creditor and/or company, directors, supervisor, magistrates' court clerk, official receiver, Secretary of State		Liquidator appointed by the court

Option 5 leads invariably to liquidation but Options 1 to 4 do not, unless the company is insolvent.

Liquidation can be voluntary or compulsory and, where business failure looks increasingly likely, professional advice should be taken sufficiently early to safeguard the option for a members' voluntary liquidation (1 below).

Type of liquidation	Instigated by	Requirements	Method
1. Voluntary a. Members'	Resolution of 75 per cent of members	Solvency	Liquidator appointed by members
b. Creditors'	Ditto	Insolvency	Liquidator appointed by members or creditors
2. Compulsory (imposed by and in some cases supervised by the court)	Creditor and/or member, company, directors, supervisor, magistrates court clerk, official receiver, Secretary of State	Members' disputes, fraud or insolvency	Application to the court

The usual order of distribution of assets by the liquidator will be:

1. Debts secured by a fixed charge
2. Winding-up expenses
3. Preferential debtors, including:

- business rate
- UK taxes (contact your accountant)
- six weeks' wages to a maximum of £184 per week
- six weeks' accrued holiday remuneration
- contributions payable under Social Security Acts and employment legislation
- 12 months' PAYE deductions

4. Debts secured by a floating charge
5. Unsecured creditors
6. Deferred creditors
7. Shareholders

167

Partnership

Type of dissolution	Instigated by	Requirements	Method
1. (a) Arrangement or moratorium with creditors (b) Voluntary liquidation	Partners	Insolvency	Application to court; partners' nominee appointed supervisor and reports to court; may not result in bankruptcy
2. Forced	Usually a creditor	Insolvency	Court proceedings for recovery of money followed by a court judgment and then appointment of a receiver or receiver and manager. And/or bankruptcy proceedings against one or more of the partners when personal assets in addition to business assets may be vulnerable
3. Selling the business	Partners	From choice, eg retirement, change of interests etc	Usually by sale of the business as a 'going concern' often including goodwill value

Partners are usually each responsible for *all* liabilities of the partnership so far as creditors are concerned. Internal sharing agreements do not affect this principle. Partnerships are best regulated by written agreement; otherwise the Partnership Act 1890 applies and some of the provisions are antiquated.

Sole trader

Procedure	Instigated by	Requirements	Method
1. Voluntary Arrangement or moratorium with creditors	Proprietor	Insolvency	Proprietor applies to court; his nominee is appointed supervisor and reports to the court – may not result in bankruptcy
2. Forced	Usually a creditor, otherwise by the proprietor on realisation of insolvency	Insolvency	Receiver appointed by the court; may result in bankruptcy
3. Selling the business	Proprietor	From choice, eg retirement, change of interests etc	Usually by sale of the business as a 'going concern' often including goodwill value

The order of distribution of assets on liquidation follows the same pattern as in the winding-up of a company except that the unsecured creditors' and deferred creditors' claims are paid after those of the preferential debtors, as partnerships and sole traders cannot borrow under a floating charge. Last to be paid are the proprietors, and partners divide any balance after distribution in accordance with their initial contribution or the terms of their partnership agreement.

Further Reading

Chapter 1

Creating Your Own Work, M Mason (Gresham Books)
Starting a Successful Small Business, M J Morris (Kogan Page)
Which Business? Stephen Halliday (Kogan Page)
Working For Yourself, Godfrey Golzen (Kogan Page)

Chapter 2

Buying a Shop, A St J Price (Kogan Page)
The Guardian Guide to Running a Small Business, Clive Woodcock (Kogan Page)
How to Buy a Business, Peter Farrell (Kogan Page)
Just for Starters, A Bollard (Intermediate Technology)
Small Beginnings, A Bollard (Intermediate Technology)
The Small Business Guide, Colin Barrow (BBC Publications)
Starting a Small Business, D Fowler (Sphere)
Taking up a Franchise, C Barrow and G Golzen (Kogan Page)
Work for Yourself, P Hall (National Extension College)

Chapter 4

Do It Yourself Advertising, Roy Brewer (Kogan Page)
Do Your Own Market Research, P N Hague and P Jackson (Kogan Page)
Effective Marketing for the Smaller Business, G Lace (Scope Books)
Getting Sales, Richard D Smith and Ginger Dick (Kogan Page)
How to Win Profitable Business, T Cannon (Hutchinson)
Managing a Sales Force, M Wilson (Gower Press)
Successful Marketing for the Small Business, Dave Patten (Kogan Page)

Chapter 5

Financial Management for the Small Business, Colin Barrow (Kogan Page)
Financing for Small Business, K Checkley (Sphere)
How to Prepare a Business Plan, Edward Blackwell (Kogan Page)
Money for Business, Bank of England
Raising Finance: The Guardian Guide for Small Business, Clive Woodcock
  (Kogan Page)

Chapter 6

Planning Permission – A Guide for Industry, HMSO

Chapter 7

Law for the Small Business, Patricia Clayton (Kogan Page)

Chapter 8

Make a Success of Micro Computing in Your Business, Parnell, Jackson & Lucas (Enterprise Books)
Simplified Book-keeping for Small Businesses, G Whitehead (Vyner)
Understand Your Accounts, A St J Price (Kogan Page)

Chapter 9

The Daily Telegraph Recruitment Handbook, Patricia Leighton (Kogan Page)
A Handbook of Personnel Management Practice, Michael Armstrong (Kogan Page)

Chapter 10

Going for Growth, Michael K Lawson (Kogan Page)
Help for Growing Business, Department of Trade and Industry
Successful Expansion for the Small Business, M J Morris (Kogan Page)

Titles related to specific businesses

Buying and Renovating Houses for Profit, K Ludman & R D Buchanan (Kogan Page)
The Kelvin Handbook of Optical Practice Development, P A Management Consultants
Running Your Own Antiques Business, Noël Riley & Godfrey Golzen (Kogan Page)
Running Your Own Boarding Kennels, Sheila Zabawa (Kogan Page)
Running Your Own Estate Agency, Val Redding (Kogan Page)
Running Your Own Hairdressing Salon, Christine Harvey & Helen Steadman (Kogan Page)
Running Your Own Mail Order Business, Malcolm Breckman (Kogan Page)
Running Your Own Photographic Business, John Rose & Linda Hankin (Kogan Page)
Running Your Own Playgroup or Nursery, Jenny Willison (Kogan Page)
Running Your Own Pub, Elven Money (Kogan Page)
Running Your Own Shop, Roger Cox (Kogan Page)
Running Your Own Small Hotel, Joy Lennick (Kogan Page)
Running Your Own Smallholding, Richard and Pauline Bambrey (Kogan Page)
Running Your Own Word Processing Service, Doreen Huntley (Kogan Page)

A full list of books about running a business is available from Kogan Page at 120 Pentonville Road, London N1 9JN.

Index